Training Families To Do a Successful Intervention

A Professional's Guide

JOHNSON INSTITUTE®

Minneapolis

Training Families To Do a Successful Intervention
A Professional's Guide

Johnson Institute-QVS, Inc.
7205 Ohms Lane
Minneapolis, MN 55439-2159
(800) 231-5165 or (612) 831-1630
E-mail: info@johnsoninstitute.com
http://www.johnsoninstitute.com

Library of Congress Cataloging-in-Publication Data
Training families to do a successful intervention: a professional's guide.
       p. cm.
    Includes bibliographical references and index.
    ISBN 1-56246-116-8
    1. Substance abuse—Treatment. 2. Crisis Intervention (Psychiatry) 3. Substance abuse—Patients—Family relationships. I. Johnson Institute (Minneapolis, Minn.)
RC564.T7285   1996
616.86'06—dc20
96-9268

CIP

Page design: Crombie Design
Cover design: Pam Belding
Printed in the United States of America

Dedication

This book is dedicated to Vernon E. Johnson, D.D., who originated the intervention process and founded the Johnson Institute.

For over thirty-five years the Johnson Institute has been committed to the integrity and constant refinement of Dr. Johnson's intervention approach—a loving process that has saved countless lives.

Acknowledgments

We extend our thanks to the following colleagues, whose advice we have taken seriously in preparing this revised and expanded version of *How to Use Intervention in Your Professional Practice*.

Members of the National Intervention Network Steering Committee:

Paul Wood, Ph.D.
Executive Director
National Council on Alcoholism and Drug Dependence (NCADD)
New York, NY

Beverly Haberle, M.H.S., CAC, CEAP
Executive Director
Bucks County Council on Alcoholism and Drug Dependence
Doylestown, PA

Myrtle Muntz, B.A., M.B.A., M.S.S.A., L.I.S.W.
President
Alcoholism Services of Cleveland, Inc.
Cleveland Heights, OH

Earl (Dick) Loomer, CEAP, RSAC
Executive Director
NCADD of Maine
Augusta, ME

K.D. Dillon, Intervention Specialist
Intervention Services
Minneapolis, MN

John P. Maloney, M.A., Certified Psychologist, CCDC
Private Practice in Addictions and Mental Health
Louisville, KY

George Perkins, Ph.D., CEAP
Executive Director
The Wellness Institute, Inc.
Louisville, KY
Member, Association of Intervention Specialists

Thanks also to Alexandra Robbin, for her dedication to clarity in written communication.

Contents

6. As a group, meet after the intervention to process the experience.

- The confrontation is accomplished without anger.
- Friends and loved ones have come together because they care.
- Comments are founded on firsthand observation—not on gossip or hearsay. Comments are limited to facts and descriptions of feelings. Blaming is not allowed.
- The main purpose of intervention is immediate action.
- Resistance is lowered as much as possible.
- The success of an intervention is not determined solely by the user's response.

- The power of loved ones
- The power of emotional dependence
- The power of an employer
- The power of law

The misuse of power

Deciding how and when to use power

Internal conflicts

The difference between guilt and shame

External conflicts

Ask yourself: What is the nature of the conflict?

The sources of delusion and denial are many:

- Blackouts
- Euphoric recall
- Repression
- Rationalizing
- Justifying and blaming
- Intellectualizing

- Minimizing
- Compensating

Anybody can get caught up in delusion and denial.

Examples of enabling and how to stop it

Spouses must stop—

Friends must stop—

Co-workers must stop—

Employers must stop—

Helping-professionals must stop—

Take care not to exaggerate the possibilities! . . .44

Chapter 2: The Role of the Professional in Intervention

When a chemically dependent person is already your client

What if *you* are a chemically dependent person in recovery?

Going it alone

Dangers of the "super counselor syndrome"

1. Help clients make a preliminary assessment of the effects the alcohol/drug use is having on all concerned.

    Ten Warning Signs of Chemical Dependence

2. Help clients look at their own use of chemicals.

3. Help clients determine where the value conflicts lie.

4. Help clients identify their strengths and weaknesses (readiness) for intervention.

Chapter 3 : A Model for Intervention Programming

Chapter 4: Questions about Intervention

FOREWORD

A message to helping-professionals from Dr. Vernon E. Johnson, founder of the Johnson Institute and father of the intervention process:

In the early 1960s, intervention was a theory that flew in the face of long-established opinion and practice. While most people were saying that nothing could be done with alcoholics until they had "hit bottom," intervention was, in fact, getting some alcoholics to accept help much earlier. And while conventional wisdom held that chemically dependent people had to be self-motivated to benefit from treatment, helpers practicing intervention were working effectively with the most resistant of addicts.

By the late 1970s, the process of intervention had gained wide acceptance. It had proved effective at every socioeconomic level in the United States.

Today we face a new challenge. Never in living memory has the abuse of alcohol and other drugs been so clearly a matter of national concern. A new term—the War on Drugs—has been added to our lexicon. It might seem that those of us who have labored long in the field would welcome this development. Yet many of us are uneasy, and some of us are distressed, by oversimplifications that lead to slogans like "Just say no" and to legislation that would stop people from abusing alcohol and other drugs—as if tougher laws and tighter enforcement can remove a deadly disease from our midst. These efforts ignore the lessons of history and obscure the true nature of chemical dependence.

When we see such misguided solutions to the problem, we're reminded of the saying,

When in danger, when in doubt,
Run in circles, scream and shout!

We seem to have succumbed to collective amnesia about what happened during the Prohibition Era (1920–1933). In the 1930s our nation came to near-consensus that the legislation had caused more problems than it had solved. But we still haven't dealt with the fact that the disease of chemical dependence renders its victims incapable of recognizing the severity of their symptoms. Addicts who are ruining their lives cannot "just say no," because they cannot—without intervention—even comprehend what drugs are doing to them. To gain insight, they need planned and caring acts of intervention—both formal and informal—from those around them.

We need to present reality in a receivable way to chemically dependent persons who are out of touch with it. We need to redirect our educational and counseling efforts to those who surround them; in other words, to mobilize concerned persons to act, and to help them become effective intervenors in the disease that is the #1 scourge of our time.

Intervention has improved the quality of life for millions of people throughout our society. For this we are grateful. And yet we know there is much more to be done.

This book gives professionals time-tested principles and techniques for guiding families and other concerned persons through the intervention process. It also presents the Johnson Institute's own intervention program model, which can be modified to suit any setting.[1]

---

[1] The Johnson Institute provides Intervention Training Seminars for helping-professionals. The seminars include practical help in adapting the program for any circumstances. Call toll-free: 1-800-231-5165.

Who can benefit from this guide?

Chemical dependence counselors, employee assistance counselors, family physicians, judges, lawyers, marriage and family therapists, nurses, probation officers, personnel directors, psychiatrists, psychologists, social workers, teachers, the clergy. We believe all helping-professionals need to know the nature of chemical dependence and the intervention process.

About terminology

Throughout this guide we use the term *alcohol/drugs* as a shortened form of *alcohol **or other** drugs*. To those who think alcohol is not a drug, we want to emphasize that it *is* a drug, just as marijuana, cocaine, "uppers," "downers," and other mind-altering substances are.

About format

This guidebook makes it easy to add your own insights to the text. The pages provide ample space for any notes you'd like to make.

CHAPTER 1

Basic Concepts of Intervention

Introduction

To understand the value of intervention, consider how it may save the life of a person whose thinking is governed by delusion and denial:[1]

> Tom, a 55-year-old machinist, had explained away symptoms of heart trouble for months—until his employer insisted on a checkup. After a thorough assessment, a team of physicians insisted that he stop smoking immediately and recommended open-heart surgery. Tom shook his head, telling his wife and his doctor not to worry; things would be all right if he could just relax a little more and smoke a little less. But of course they were worried, and so they tried to convince him with test results and statistics. His wife begged him to do the right thing. He wouldn't listen. Only after Tom's entire family and his employer met with him face-to-face, expressing their concerns—and describing how

[1] Delusion: Being out of touch with the reality that a problem exists. Denial: Consciously or unconsciously not admitting that the problem is as serious as it is. Not facing the fact that one's behavior is hurting oneself and others. A defense mechanism to avoid uncomfortable feelings and to protect one's sense of security.

his refusal to take care of himself affected their own lives—did Tom face the reality of his condition and accept the necessary help.

Marsha, a 45-year-old real estate broker, was bluntly told by her physician that if she didn't stop drinking, it would kill her. For years her husband, Allen, had been pleading with her to quit and threatening to walk out if she didn't. (Still he had covered for her at work, phoning in countless reasons she had to be absent or tardy.) Marsha's children, now in their teens, had created their own ways of coping with her behavior. When the doctor phoned Allen to say it was a matter of life and death, Allen finally sought referral to a counselor. Fortunately the counselor was well trained in intervention. Allen got solid information—some of which he had never heard, some of which he had heard but ignored. The counselor talked with the children as well.

Allen and the children received more than information. They learned about their power as individuals and their collective strength as a family. *They also learned how to focus that power and strength* on helping Marsha to stop her drinking. The method: a carefully planned family intervention, in which Marsha would receive support while being confronted with uncomfortable facts about how her drinking was causing problems for everyone else at home and at work—and what the people affected by her drinking thought about it and how they felt about it (mad, sad, and scared).

What do these cases have in common? A person faced with serious illness refuses to admit—or even to believe—that the problem is real and must be dealt with.

Medical advice and the pleas and threats of a loved one are ignored. It requires the concerted effort of those who care about the person to break through the walls of delusion and denial and prompt the person to accept help. The pain level is raised so high it outweighs the fear of entering treatment.

Are all interventions essentially the same?

During our lifetime there may be many occasions when we must tell people how their actions are hurting them or impinging on us, so that they will stop. As difficult as it may be, we know that if we don't step in, the behavior will continue. This is probably the most familiar meaning of intervention.

In regard to chemical dependence, intervention has a particular meaning because of the nature of the problem. Chemical dependence is an insidious illness that creeps up on a person, creating denial and eventually self-delusion about the reality and seriousness of the situation. The person who has grown dependent on alcohol or another mind-altering drug is not the only one whose thinking has become distorted by denial and delusion. Those who are closest to that person also lose touch with the reality of the situation. Chemical dependence ensnares the user— and those who are close—into a self-destructive system of feeling, thinking, and behaving.

A major task of the helping-professional is to break through that tightly bound system of defenses so that those who care about the user can take effective action to help him or her *and to help themselves*. This requires more than "stepping in." Because of the nature of chemical dependence, a successful intervention must include both confrontation (about facts, followed by feelings) and support.

Whom are the interventions for?

Clearly intervention is for the sake of the chemically dependent person. But it's also for the sake of family members, close friends, coworkers, and others who are affected by that person's drinking or using. The intervenors need to know they have done all they can. They also need to know they have the power—and the right—to improve their own lives, even if the user chooses not to get help.

Breaking through defenses

A well-planned intervention is systematic, not piecemeal. But when use of a chemical is causing harm to the user and others, here are some things that can be done by concerned persons in the absence of a structured intervention:

Describe the behavior. The one giving feedback need not be a family member, a coworker, or even a close friend. Any concerned associate can take the initiative.

Whoever gives the feedback must be clear about it. How did the person look while drinking? How did the person sound? Exactly what did the person do? Whose feelings were affected, and how? Whose safety was endangered, and how?

Bruce, you've been a special part of my life and Ginnie's life for a long time. But last night you put Ginnie in danger by driving under the influence. That really scared me, and it hurt me too, to think you would do a thing like that. You may not remember, but you slurred your words, and you stumbled off the curb when you walked back to your car. I don't want you to drive her home when you've been drinking.

Plan to confront when the person is not drinking or high, so that the confrontation will be felt and remembered.

Describe your feelings. Concerned relatives, friends, and coworkers can tell the chemically dependent person how they've been hurt, frightened, saddened, angered, or embarrassed by certain behavior. *Without a description of feelings, there is no intervention.* Without a description of feelings, the user interprets everything as judgment, ganging up, conspiracy, and general animosity.

State only what you yourself have experienced in relation to the person's drinking/using and what you yourself have felt.

Betty, I think you're an intelligent and thoughtful woman. You've always been sensitive to other people's feelings. But at the restaurant last night, I saw how you changed as you continued to drink before dinner. You became more and more irritable. You were loud and rude to the server. Nothing was right. I was embarrassed—but mainly I felt sad. I feel as if I'm losing my friend.

Be loving, yet aware of your anger so that you can control it. In describing the user's behavior and your feelings about that behavior, avoid an accusatory tone.

Not this: I hate what you did to me at the office party.

This: When you were drunk at the office party, you turned around and spilled your drink on my boss's new dress. Then you made a comment that she could easily afford a new one, considering how little she pays me. I felt horrified; I just felt like crawling into a hole.

Stop enabling. Many of us are inclined to protect the person who is drunk, high, or hung over. We clean up messes, prevent accidents, "cover" with lies to friends and coworkers, show sympathy, make excuses, or look the other way. But in so doing, we lift responsibility from the person's own shoulders. We interfere with the logical consequences of the person's behavior.

This interference is a form of *enabling*. In effect, an enabler is an unwitting participant in the destructive behavior, adding to the certainty that it will continue.

At a breakfast meeting with coworkers, Mike mentioned that he'd had a terrible time with his girlfriend over the weekend. He'd gotten drunk and yelled at her in the lobby of her high-rise about 2:00 A.M. on Saturday. Someone called the police, but Mike wasn't arrested. When he said maybe he should do something about his drinking, all but one person at the table laughed it off, saying, "Forget it! We all have a bad night now and then." Just one person said maybe Mike did have something to worry about and encouraged him to talk with the employee assistance counselor. Mike went on to make an appointment.

Stop accepting apologies. Letting yourself be imposed on this way is another form of enabling.

> Bill was an alcoholic with many years in A.A.— and many slips. After rude behavior toward friends while drinking, it was customary for him to call each one and apologize. He'd say, "You know I wouldn't have done that if I hadn't been drinking." And each time they would reassure him: "Of course not, Bill. Don't worry about it." But this time his friend Joe was forthright. "Bill, you and I have known each other for a long time. It's true that when you're drinking, you don't really know how it affects you. But I want you to know how it affects me. More than once you've made crude remarks about my wife. This hurts. I know it's hard to choose not to drink. But it's not all right to insult someone I love. I want to support you in staying with the program." Much later—when Bill had more than a year's sobriety—he admitted to Joe that this confrontation had prompted him do what he knew he had to do.

Offer help and support. Many resources—both professional and self-help—are ready to assist people suffering from chemical dependence. Find out what qualified help is available and specifically how to get it.[2] (See also *Why make treatment the major focus of intervention?* and *What are the qualities of an excellent treatment program?* in Chapter 4.) Make yourself available to carry through.

> Frank, you and I have been friends for a long time. I worry about what alcohol is doing to

---

[2] The National Council on Alcoholism and Drug Dependence (NCADD) can assist. Write them at 12 West 21st Street, New York, NY 10010; or phone (212) 206-6770. You may also call the Johnson Institute: 1-800-231-5165.

your life—and I know that you worry too, because you've told me several times that you're afraid you're drinking too much on weekends. The Lake County Clinic has a good reputation for helping people with drinking problems. I've made an appointment for us to look into it next Tuesday evening at 6:00. Let's go see what they have to offer.

Be consistent. Be relevant. Straightforward confrontations by one friend or loved one can work, although it's usually more effective to involve as many as possible. If each caring person would continually and consistently describe the drunken or high behavior and how it affects everyone concerned, it's likely that more users would seek help and stay with it.

Most important, the messages must be *consistent* and *relevant*. If a spouse says the problem is serious but a close friend later disagrees, the spouse's intervention probably won't work. And when concerned persons offer useless advice like "What you need is willpower; you're not trying hard enough," they're offering no help at all.

Stay true to yourself. This is related to consistency. Whether or not the person stops using alcohol/drugs, you must decide how to conduct the rest of your own life— and then follow through. If, for example, you decide you'll end your marriage if the using continues, you must say so and then stick to your resolution. If you decide that you'll dismiss an employee if the quality of work continues to slide, you must say exactly what needs improvement and then fire the person if standards are not met. To go back on your word will merely *enable* the unacceptable behavior to continue, adding to your misery.

The six steps of an effective intervention

The terms *structured intervention, family intervention,* and, simply, *intervention* refer to the carefully planned, methodical process and techniques of getting a chemically dependent person to accept the needed help.

The following model of intervention was developed by Dr. Vernon E. Johnson, founder of the Johnson Institute. In his book *Intervention: How to Help Someone Who Doesn't Want Help, a Step-by-Step Guide for Families and Friends of Chemically Dependent Persons,*[3] Dr. Johnson explains the process and its clinical foundation.

Frustrated by his own and other counselors' inability to get alcoholics to examine the effects their drinking had on themselves and the people they cared about, Dr. Johnson in 1962 embarked on a five-year study. The responses of 200 recovering alcoholics led him to a quantum leap in understanding: **Crisis, rather than spontaneous insight, was the key to recovery.** All of the recovering alcoholics had experienced crises in many areas of their lives, related directly to their drinking. The crises had finally forced them to recognize and deal with their alcoholism.

Dr. Johnson and his colleagues wondered why they had to wait for such crises to build up. *Why couldn't they use crises creatively to initiate an intervention?*

After trying various approaches, they decided that the most effective one was *to gather concerned relatives and*

---

[3] Published by the Johnson Institute. (See Appendix C, *Johnson Institute Resources for Programming.*) For more information call toll-free: 1-800-231-5165.

friends of the alcoholic and help them present reality in a receivable way to the alcoholic. In other words, the relatives and friends would describe the facts of the disease: specifically how the person behaved while intoxicated; how they felt when this happened; how family relationships, job performance, and health were affected; and other pertinent observations. These facts would be presented in a nonjudgmental, caring manner so that the alcoholic could hear them, rather than tune them out.

With further development, this breakthrough led to the *six steps of an effective intervention*:

1. Call a meeting of concerned people who are especially meaningful to the user.

2. Have participants make lists describing specific incidents of drinking/using and how they felt about each incident.

3. Have participants decide on the specific treatment plan they expect the user to accept.

4. Have participants decide exactly what they will do if the user rejects all forms of help.

5. As a group, meet with the user to present the information and the proposed treatment plan.

6. As a group, meet after the intervention to process the experience.

1. Call a meeting of concerned people who are especially meaningful to the user.

They might be family members, close friends, coworkers, physicians, and clergy. They must know *firsthand* how use of the chemical has affected the person. They need to have witnessed accidents, threats, verbal or physical lashing out, embarrassing behavior, reckless spending, drunk driving, stealing, blackouts, lies, broken promises, tardiness or absence, falling grades, lowered productivity, job loss, poor grooming, poor housekeeping, physical illness, lawsuits, arrests, lost opportunities, lost friendships, or other *specific incidents or changes* related to the person's use of alcohol/drugs.

In this group, do not include anyone who believes chemical dependence is a sign of personal weakness or moral depravity.

Do include those who cannot attend the structured intervention in person. If it's possible and reasonable to do so, arrange to present any videotapes or audiotapes the absent persons have made. (The tapes would be played during both the rehearsal and the actual intervention.)[4] Take as much care in guiding preparation of the tapes as you do in preparation for the direct presentations.

What about including children and grandparents? Because of their ability to tap parental instincts, children can be especially powerful.[5] Yet they are extremely vulnerable to inappropriate and unwarranted pressure. In consultation with those responsible for the child's welfare, a qualified professional must carefully weigh the risks and benefits and decide whether participation would be healthful. (See also step 5.)

Grandparents and other respected older adults may also be especially influential.

---

[4] Use your judgment about presenting video/audiotapes from those who are too dysfunctional to attend the sessions. Be sure you have their written permission to do so.

[5] It's usually appropriate and effective to include children aged ten and older.

2. Have participants make lists describing specific incidents of drinking/using and how they felt about each incident.

Only firsthand knowledge is allowed; gossip and hearsay are not. Neither are generalities like "You're drinking too much." Each description must be specific.

After describing an incident, participants describe how it affected their own feelings and behavior and how it has affected their relationship with the user. For example,

What I've observed	How it has affected my feelings & behavior	How it has affected our relationship

After the specifics, observations of general changes in the user's behavior, personality, attitude, motivation, and character (moral/ethical choices) may be added.

All observations must be worded simply, in a caring manner—not hostile, accusatory, or condescending.

NOTE: Some professional interventionists have participants prepare letters, rather than lists. (Lists still help the writers compose their letters.) These interventionists say a letter flows more naturally when read aloud, and that it sounds more compassionate than a list. Other interventionists have found that lists, crisp and to the point, work better than flowing letters.

3. Have participants decide on the specific treatment plan they expect the user to accept.

Before meeting with the user, those concerned must decide exactly what help they think is needed. The aim is to get the person to start the course of action *immediately* upon conclusion of the meeting.

Given the realities of managed health care, what sort of help is ideal? Most preferred is primary treatment (inpatient or outpatient) at a reputable facility. Other options include group therapy or counseling by a qualified Chemical Dependence Specialist; also Twelve-Step recovery groups such as Alcoholics Anonymous, Cocaine Anonymous, or Narcotics Anonymous.

If most users attend A.A. or a similar program after treatment, why not save time and money by going there directly from intervention? Because Twelve-Step programs are very effective *for those who remain in the fellowship*. Receiving primary treatment before entering such a group will, we believe, increase the probability that the chemically dependent person will stay in the fellowship and fully recover.

Some intervention counselors are willing to employ "what if" clauses; others are not. A "what if" clause is used when the using person refuses to accept the presented course of action without trying his or her own plan first. In such cases those concerned may say, "All right, you can try it your way. But we want you to agree *now* that if you start drinking again, you'll immediately start the program we have presented."

A "what if" clause can be risky, because when the user resumes drinking/using, she or he will not consider the agreement as valid. A "what if" clause should be used only if there is no other way to get movement. What's important is that the user has made a commitment to positive action if the drinking/using resumes. (See *What about "what if" clauses?* in task 3 of *Structuring the intervention,* in Chapter 2.)

4. Have participants decide exactly what they will do if the user rejects all forms of help.

A spouse, for example, might decide to say, "If you don't accept treatment, I will not subject the children or myself to living with your cocaine use any longer." An employer might decide to say, "We aren't recommending your *best* alternative; we're presenting your *only* alternative. I, for one, have already given you too many chances. This is your last one. If you want to keep your job, you'll do what we recommend."

But it won't always be necessary to state the "bottom line." Often the observations of behavior and the descriptions of feelings are so convincing that help is accepted and even requested. To go further may be overkill. (Stating the bottom line can be effective later, should the person want to leave the treatment program.)

5. As a group, meet with the user to present the information and the proposed treatment plan.

A caring, respectful, nonjudgmental, nonpatronizing approach is crucial to the intervention process. Those who cannot control their anger and resentment should *not* attend this meeting. (Expressing the anger and working through it should come later, during treatment—ideally in a structured family counseling program.)

Anyone who may try to gain compliance through intimidation or coercion should not attend this meeting, either.

Nor should those (often parents and grandparents) who don't want to "kick him when he's down." Instead they might be asked to support those who do participate, or to support a successful outcome. If those who refuse to attend the intervention session are not provided a constructive role and encouraged to feel they're part of the team—and if the intervention then fails—they might start casting blame.

What about including children? In consultation with those responsible for the child's welfare, a qualified professional must carefully decide whether speaking up in the session would be healthful. The child's age and emotional condition should be carefully considered. An alternative may be to present a videotape/audiotape or to have a group member read the child's handwritten letter. It's important not to set the stage for an accusation that the child has been coerced.

6. As a group, meet after the intervention to process the experience.

Because it offers team members a chance to process their feelings, the post-intervention session can be the most significant step of the entire intervention. Too often, after investing themselves in a lot of hard work and exposing their own pain, the intervenors are left hanging while the user goes on to treatment. If the user accepted help before everyone had a chance to present their information, the ones who missed out are left hanging as well.

This is the time for the facilitator to give everyone a chance to process what happened during the session and to help them develop a plan of action for their own recovery. When the facilitator affords everyone this opportunity, it can be said that the intervention has been a success even if the user has refused any help. It has been a success because all the concerned persons involved in the process have learned from the experience and have had a chance to do something *for themselves*. Family dynamics have changed for the better.

In the event that the user has refused every alternative, it's also important to reassure those who did not participate—for whatever reason—that the user's decision is not their fault.

Why does structured intervention work?

To understand why the intervention session is so effective in getting the chemically dependent person to face reality and accept help, contrast it with the nagging, threats, and other negative approaches the person has heard in the past. It's different from anything the user has had to face during years of alcohol/drug use. It's hard to defend oneself when criticism is expressed in a caring way.

The confrontation is accomplished without anger.

You may think it dishonest for family and friends to express care and understanding when what they'd really like to do is vent their rage. But experience has proved *it is not effective to express anger* during a structured intervention.

When the user arrives at the initial meeting, it's with the dread of being attacked. When the attack does not happen—that is, *when the expectation of anger is overturned*—it's so surprising that the person is usually rendered open to hearing the truth. A transformation is allowed to begin.

Friends and loved ones have come together because they care.

How often in our lives do family or friends gather to tell us they love us and are concerned about our welfare? How often do they honestly tell us how we may be harming ourselves or someone else—and then make themselves available to help change the situation? Rarely or not at all.

This is what makes the process of intervention so powerful. One alcoholic in treatment described how it had affected him:

> I knew deep down what my drinking was doing
> to me. I don't think I knew or could have

known, though, that so many people were genuinely concerned about my drinking. Sure, they were upset about how my drinking was affecting their lives. But mostly they were concerned about what it was doing to me. That really shook me.

Comments are founded on firsthand observation—not on gossip or hearsay. Comments are limited to facts and descriptions of feelings. Blaming is not allowed.

Chemically dependent persons who continue to use alcohol/drugs are prepared to fight back when confronted with generalities, moral judgments, accusations, and even facts without feelings. But they are not prepared to refute specifics, clearly stated without rancor, from friends and loved ones who care. They cannot refute a concerned person's genuine feelings. For this reason many once-skeptical counselors have come to believe the alcoholic who says, "I didn't realize what my drinking was doing to other people or to me. I didn't really understand."

The main purpose of intervention is immediate action.

The main goal is to get the user to let down defenses enough to (a) see what the use of alcohol/drugs is doing to self and others, (b) listen to the recommended treatment plan, and (c) accept help without delay.

Contrast this with the lectures, threats, and well-meaning advice the user has probably shut out in the past. Although the structured intervention session is brief, its clarity and its determined, positive approach make it an ideal introduction to a long-term plan for change. Having a well-conceived action plan ready to go at the moment the user is most open is crucial.

The second purpose of intervention is to provide concerned persons a chance to say to themselves, "I did everything I could to help." This message is essential for lifting burdens of guilt and self-imposed responsibility, allowing concerned persons to get on with their own recovery.

Resistance is lowered as much as possible.

All bases are covered: The key people (loved and/or respected by the user) are there, and so the user is less likely to ask someone else for a second opinion. The presentation is surprising—unlike anything the user has ever heard before. By upsetting expectations, it renders the person's usual defenses unworkable. A plan of action is ready. All this comes together at once. The collective power of family and friends has been mobilized, closing the escape hatch.

If the action plan is not thoroughly prepared—as usually happens when laypersons or helping-professionals intervene without a trained facilitator—the session is far less likely to be effective.

The success of an intervention is not determined solely by the user's response.

The person who comes to you for help is not likely to be the one who is chemically dependent. It will probably be a member of the user's family, perhaps including close friends. If they are able to gain the awareness, courage, and skill to participate in a structured intervention session, that in itself is a therapeutic success. The participants will have changed their own lives in a major way—and will have made an impression on the user, whether or not it's ever acknowledged.

Remember that one aim of intervention is to begin putting a stop to *enabling*. The user is only one member of an *enabling system* composed of family, friends, coworkers, and others who—through action or inaction—are unwittingly helping to perpetuate the problem. The structured intervention is the beginning of a process of dismantling the system. It is not a single event for the sole benefit of the user.

An individual recovery plan must be developed for each person close to the user, so that the process of recovery can continue for everyone beyond the initial confrontation.

The dynamics of intervention

What are the elements of the dynamic tension that makes effective intervention possible? Consider the interaction of

A. Power

B. Value conflicts

C. Delusion and denial

D. Enabling

E. Systematic resistance

A. Power

While preparing for the intervention session, participants must come to understand the power they possess individually and collectively. They must also decide what power they are willing to use.

Frequently those who are close to the user don't know their own restorative power, because they have developed codependent traits or even a codependent personality disorder.[6] Others concerned about the user may be so enmeshed in their own patterns of denial, delusion, and enabling that they cannot see or use the power available to them.

It's also common for concerned persons to think that any power they may have is compromised or exceeded by the power of the user. Before treatment, for example, an alcoholic may be very dependent on his wife emotionally; yet she may fail to understand how important this is, because she feels a keen lack of economic power. ("If I confront him about his drinking, he'll probably leave. I don't know what I would do. I don't have any job skills. He could take the kids away from me.")

Empowerment is essential if the intervenors are to think clearly and reclaim health for themselves. In an intervention session, to describe reality is to exert one's power. To accept one's part in perpetuating a problem— and to be willing to change—is a sign of good health.

The *power to intervene* comes in different forms, from different sources:

---

[6] By "codependent" we mean a person who is psychologically and/or emotionally dysfunctional as a result of a close, dependent relationship with a chemically dependent person. Codependents tend to be as deluded about the alcohol/drug use as the user—and, despite unpleasant consequences, they persist in enabling the user to continue using. (For more about codependence, see *The concerned persons group* in Chapter 3.)

- **The power of loved ones**

  When a chemically dependent person understands that his or her alcohol/drug use has been hurting a loved one, this may be enough to get the person to accept help. Loved ones tend to assume that the user already knows how they've been hurt—but that assumption may be wrong. Although the user has probably heard complaints, psychological defenses have minimized them (made them seem less serious) in order to protect the self from the pain others are suffering. It's also common for users to forget how many times they have hurt someone. The structured intervention lays out clearly the particular and cumulative effects that the alcohol/drug use has had on those who are most meaningful to the user.

  What about using the power of a child? See step 5 of *The six steps of an effective intervention*, earlier in this chapter.

- **The power of emotional dependence**

  Face-to-face with the fact that their behavior is hurting others, some users are not moved to accept help. This apparent indifference does not necessarily mean the user doesn't care. It might mean the user cannot cope with the realization that loved ones have been hurt. It might signify an overwhelming fear of living without drinking/using. The remedy for this turning away may be to convince the user that the relationship is in jeopardy. The person may be moved only by the likelihood of losing a dependent relationship. A husband, for example, may tune out when his wife describes how he has hurt her—but may sit up and listen when he senses he's about to lose her because she will no longer *tolerate* their hurtful, codependent relationship. Exerting power does not necessarily mean leaving the relationship. It can mean building a healthy new one:

> John, I care deeply about the problems alcohol is causing in our lives, and so I'm going to quit covering them up. I will call your boss if you want, but this time I'll say you're too sick from a hangover— not that you have the flu. I don't want to protect your drinking anymore. I love you and want things to be different for us. And I want all of us to get help.

- **The power of an employer**

  Finding out that one's employer is fed up and no longer willing to *tolerate* certain behavior can prompt a user to accept treatment. For some the fear of job loss can be as motivating as the fear of losing family or friends. The facts need not be stated directly by the employer/boss/supervisor. In fact, for the sake of personal privacy during the intervention session, it's usually more appropriate for a close coworker to describe the risks the person is facing on the job and then pledge to stop *enabling* at work—making excuses, pretending not to notice, taking over the user's responsibilities, and in other ways protecting the user from the consequences of being impaired. (See *Enabling* later in this chapter.)

- **The power of law**

  Sometimes it's appropriate and necessary for the parents of a minor—or the close relatives of an adult—to sign court commitment papers to force the user into treatment. Commitment laws vary from state to state. Orders are usually reserved for users in immediate danger of physically harming themselves or others. People convicted of drunk driving and other crimes involving the use of alcohol/drugs ordinarily forfeit some rights to self-determination. They may be required to accept treatment for chemical dependence. Here the power of law lies in the hands of judges, prosecutors, probation officers, and other professionals in law enforcement, court services, and corrections.

The misuse of power

If its purpose is to shame or coerce the chemically dependent person into treatment, the use of power is inappropriate and ineffective. A user's husband, for example, may be wise *not* to use the leverage of emotional dependence (such as a statement that he will leave if she continues drinking because he knows how emotionally threatening that would be). He may be wiser to limit his statements to descriptions of her behavior and his feelings about that behavior. If his wife already understands that he will leave if she continues drinking, she doesn't need to be threatened with an ultimatum in the group. A user's probation officer is wiser to help the client seek treatment than to force it by order of the court.

Deciding how and when to use power

Remember the interacting elements that make an effective intervention possible: **power, value conflicts, delusion and denial, enabling,** and **systematic resistance.**

Not every bit of power available to intervenors should be used in the session. There is no need to be heavy-handed. How and when to use the various forms of power will depend on where the *value conflicts* lie.

B. Value conflicts: internal and external

The leverage that can be used to get a person into treatment will vary according to the nature of the person's value system. The person with a highly developed conscience is different from one whose conscience is minimal or immature. The person of conscience has an internal sense of right and wrong. This person experiences normal (or exaggerated) feelings of guilt for real (or imagined) harm done to others. The person with minimal or no conscience lacks a sense of right and wrong and therefore has little or no feeling of guilt for hurting others.

Internal conflicts

For the chemically dependent person of conscience, internal value conflicts create feelings of great discomfort. They arise from a sense of right and wrong and empathy for other living beings.

Intervention is most likely to be successful when the user is experiencing some internal conflict. Feelings of guilt upon hearing how actions have embarrassed or hurt others may be enough to prompt the person to accept treatment. To apply additional power/leverage (such as the threat of job loss, jail, or legal action for a court-ordered commitment) may be unnecessary, humiliating, and counterproductive. The helping-professional, with the aid of those who are closest to the user, needs to evaluate carefully the guilt or shame the user is feeling.

The difference between guilt and shame. It's important for all intervenors to understand the difference between guilt and shame.

Guilt is feeling remorseful about doing something wrong. It's a normal, necessary, and usually healthful emotion. Guilt *before* the fact (imagining how sorry we would be) helps us put on the brakes and set boundaries on our behavior. Feeling guilty *after* the fact provides "a way back," a way to make amends, a way to heal the hurt we've inflicted, through restitution. Guilt says, "I've *done* something bad." It helps us mobilize ourselves to change.

Shame, on the other hand, is immobilizing. It speaks to our soul, condemning us. Withering statements like "Shame on you! How can you be so stupid?" and "Only an idiot or a crazy person would do what you did!" give us no way back from our transgressions. They stand in the way of our making things right. Shame leads a person to think, "I *am* bad." Each time we hear how worthless we are, our power and desire to change are diminished. People who have repeatedly been shamed begin to believe they really are crazy, stupid, or bad.

External conflicts

External value conflicts create feelings of discomfort not within the user, but within those who are affected by the user's behavior. The people affected typically focus on a "need to change the chemically dependent person."

Whatever their age, some users feel no internal conflict about the harm their behavior is doing to self and others. They're not bothered by guilt or the disapproval of family and friends. Like young children with immature conscience development—or like sociopathic adults—

they refrain from certain behavior only because they fear being caught and punished.

Chemically dependent teenagers—young adults— who identify with peer groups engaged in alcohol/drug use often feel no conflict about it. To them, chemical use is the norm. Their actions are strongly influenced by external forces, and so external power is the type needed to bring their behavior under control.

Adult users with histories of sociopathic behavior and an apparent lack of normal conscience usually respond only to application of external power, such as the readiness of family members, probation officers, and the court to pursue commitment or incarceration.

Ask yourself: What is the nature of the conflict?

In an ideal intervention, all participants have a conscience and are capable of feeling internal conflict and guilt. This makes it easier for family members to review their shared values (in steps 1 and 2) and to present them to the user (in step 5), embarking on a mutual journey, with everyone getting help.

If the chemically dependent person feels no internal conflict while family members feel the turmoil of external conflict, the family will have to use all the external power/leverage available to it.

Sometimes there is no apparent conflict of values— either internal or external—among family members. For example, if one family member goes to jail on a third DWI and the others respond by calling it police harassment, the conflict is external to both the user and the rest of the family. When there is no significant conflict of values within the family, the power to intervene will probably have to be imposed from outside. Child-protection services, for example, may have to pressure the parents of a chemically dependent adolescent; or a judge may have to pressure an adult convicted of drunk driving. The disadvantage of outside pressure to accept treatment is that it creates fear and consternation in the family while increasing the power of the user.

C. Delusion and denial

We have seen how **power** and **internal/external value conflicts** must be considered in any intervention. Other elements are **delusion and denial, enabling,** and **systematic resistance**.

Delusion and *denial* are mental mechanisms that become the cornerstone of chemical dependence. Long after serious consequences of alcohol/drug dependence have affected the user—and the user's family, coworkers, and friends—delusion and denial continue to support the use of the mind-altering chemicals. Delusion and denial characterize not only the user, but also anyone who is codependent and anyone else who enables the user to escape logical consequences.

Delusion is a thought process that allows a user to believe things are going all right.

My job performance is great.

Everyone at the party thought my jokes were hilarious.

My kids are doing fine.

I'm still a good driver when I've had a few drinks.

I can quit tomorrow if I want to.

Denial is a defense mechanism that protects a user from realizing the hurt and pain other people are feeling because of the addicted behavior. Through denial, one negates the fact that one's addiction or codependence is hurting someone else.

To intervene effectively, it's not important to memorize distinctions between delusion and denial. The processes are fused, as in the following scenario:

> Simone, a wealthy, well-groomed woman about 60 years old, sat in the office of the county attorney, watching a videotape recorded as the state patrol picked her up for drunk driving. The tape clearly showed Simone staggering as she tried to walk a straight line and missing the mark as she tried to touch her finger to her nose. On the audio portion of the tape, she slurred her words and couldn't complete a coherent sentence. But as she watched and listened, she shook her head in disbelief. "That's not me," she insisted. "That is not me!"

Delusion and denial push the chemically dependent person deeper and deeper into the disease process. It gets to the point where the truth about the alcohol/drug use is virtually inaccessible—until it's presented concretely and powerfully through a structured intervention.

The sources of delusion and denial are many:

- **Blackouts**

  A blackout is a chemically induced period of amnesia in which experiences fail to reach long-term memory. It is not the same as passing out; the drinker who passes out appears to fall asleep abruptly. During a blackout the person is conscious, even animated. A blackout may last for seconds, minutes, hours, or even days, during which the drinker is active but storing no memories of the activities. Many alcoholics have been surprised to see what they have done—both routine and bizarre—with no recollection of having done them. Many have awakened in the morning to discover they've put their children, pets, or property in harm's way. Many have awakened in terror, unable to recall what happened the night before. It's not uncommon to check the car to make sure it's not dented or to see whether it's parked in its usual place. Finding the car safely parked, and with no memory of any incident, the drinker remains in delusion and denial.

- **Euphoric recall**

  Another source of delusion and denial is the tendency to remember only the good times and good feelings one has had while high. It's usually accompanied by the impression that one's performance while intoxicated is exceptionally fine, when in fact it is poor and even inappropriate.

  > Late one morning after a big party, Jason sauntered into the kitchen, chuckling. As he sat down for coffee, he reminded his partner how well he had played the saxophone and how witty he had been with the hosts. His partner, Chris, looked stunned. In reality Chris was embarrassed about the drinks Jason had spilled on the couch, the jokes he had made about the food, the obscene stories he had told, and

the way he had disrupted the party by blaring his saxophone.

- **Repression**

  According to some theories of human behavior, repression is a process by which unacceptable thoughts (ideas, feelings, and memories) are buried in a person's unconscious. The more painful or repugnant they are, the more deeply they're buried. For example, memories and desires that contradict a person's sense of decency will not be allowed to surface. Because repressed thoughts are not conscious, they can lead to unintentional behavior that resembles action during a blackout. When, for instance, an alcoholic is told that after a night of drinking he made a pass at the baby-sitter while driving her home, his shock may be genuine, his shame very real. Repression keeps painful facts out of awareness—laying the groundwork for delusion and denial.

- **Rationalizing**

  Human beings have a need to make sense of the world. This need is so great that we sometimes alter reality to make it make sense. For example, when we're criticized, we usually try to explain ourselves. When faced with certain tasks, we invent reasons for avoiding them. We try to make our behavior seem sensible to other people and we do the same thing in "inner conversation" with ourselves. To turn something unacceptable into something acceptable, we rationalize. We tell ourselves why we will or won't; why we did or didn't; why we should or shouldn't; or why somebody else will or won't, did or didn't, should or shouldn't. Rationalizing is chronic among users, codependents, and enablers. It leads to, and supports, both delusion and denial.

> Dreading a major presentation to clients, Dana told herself, "If I get too nervous and blow it, we'll be in deep trouble. A couple of drinks should steady my nerves and be good for both me and the company."

- **Justifying and blaming**

Like rationalizing, these are ways to explain and excuse the use of alcohol/drugs and the resulting problems.

> If you had responsibilities like mine, you'd drink too.

> I only get out of town once in a while. It doesn't hurt to tie one on at a convention.

> If Tom hadn't been late meeting me for dinner, I wouldn't have had those extra drinks.

> My boss has been waiting for an excuse to get rid of me.

- **Intellectualizing**

To explain their use of alcohol/drugs, some users cite complex psycho-social factors.

> I'm a sensitive, artistic person who feels the pain of the world too strongly. Marijuana mellows me out so I can stand it.

Some of the best novelists of our time have done their best work with a bottle of Scotch at their elbow.

Coleridge used opium. I'm a poet, so why shouldn't I use cocaine?

- **Minimizing**

To make their behavior seem less serious, some chemically dependent persons minimize it.

Sure, I had a few drinks, but it's nothing to get upset about. The other guys had a lot more than I did.

Calm down! I knew what I was doing. That truck was a good ten feet away from us.

People close to the user often minimize too: "If he can drink heavily and still get to work, things can't be so bad." Minimizing reinforces delusion and denial.

- **Compensating**

A worker who relies on alcohol/drugs may slack off for a length of time and then, with exceptional effort, accomplish a task quite well—obscuring the fact that job performance has deteriorated. The ability to compensate for periods of feeling hung-over and strung-out maintains the delusion that no problem exists. "That's one hell of a report I produced. And they think I have a drinking problem! This will show them how wrong they are."

Anybody can get caught up in delusion and denial.
Those concerned about the chemically dependent person—including professionals—can unwittingly engage in the rationalizing, justifying, excusing, blaming, intellectualizing, minimizing, and other actions that support delusion and denial. Life partners seem especially prone to accept the user's version of reality, rather than trust their own view of what is really going on.

Delusion and denial can become so interwoven in the family life of a chemically dependent person that it's difficult for a helping-professional to identify all the strands. In the process, the professional must be careful not to agree with those who rationalize, justify, excuse, blame, intellectualize, or minimize unhealthy behavior. In other words, the interventionist must guard against *enabling*, which invites and supports more delusion and denial.

D. Enabling

Delusion and denial are fostered every time someone shields a user from the logical consequences of alcohol/drug use. For example, when a wife takes responsibility for waking up her husband, shaking him out of bed, helping him get dressed, and calling his supervisor with an excuse for his tardiness, she is reinforcing the delusion that life can continue this way without serious consequences. She is *enabling* the behavior, ensuring that it will get worse. When a friend reassures the husband that it's silly to feel guilty about missing work once in a while because of a hangover, the friend is *enabling*—and fostering denial that anyone else may be suffering because of his absence.

The helping-professional needs to bring each concerned person to full awareness of the many ways enabling happens and how to stop it. Because enabling is nearly always unwitting and unintentional, each person must also be helped not to feel guilty about having done it.

Examples of enabling and how to stop it

Until they become acutely aware of *enabling*, family members, friends, coworkers, employers, and even helping-professionals unwittingly encourage the addict's use of alcohol/drugs. To stop enabling, everyone associated with the user must stop doing things like the following:

Spouses must stop

- Covering; making excuses and lying to friends, relatives, the children, and the user's employer

- Subordinating self and forfeiting fun to accommodate the wishes of the user; for example, turning down invitations to parties where alcohol will not be served

- Keeping up appearances; making sure that the user looks neat and properly dressed

- Taking responsibility for the user; making sure the user gets to work

- Doing all the household chores, including those that the user did in the past

- Disposing of caches of alcohol/drugs

- Taking care of the user who is sick from alcohol/drugs; cleaning up vomit and other messes

- Consoling the user who is moping about problems brought on by the use of alcohol/drugs

Friends must stop

- Looking the other way; pretending not to notice

- Acting entertained; making light of the user's behavior while drunk or high

- Covering; doing the user's work; making excuses for certain behavior

- Assuring the user that everything is fine, or that others are exaggerating the problem

- Joining the user in consuming alcohol/drugs

- Consoling the user; blaming others for problems caused by the alcohol/drug use

- Riding in a car with any driver who has been drinking or who is under the influence of another drug

Coworkers must stop

- Doing the work of the user; helping the user finish tasks

- Covering up the user's mistakes and poor performance; making excuses

- Lying to the supervisor about the user's absence during the work day

- Making excuses to the user's living companion; exaggerating the pressure the user is under

- Looking the other way; pretending not to notice

- Joining the user in a drink after work; teasing the user for ordering a nonalcoholic beverage; buying drinks; keeping up with the amount the user consumes; betting who can drink the most

- Assuring the user that certain behavior is normal; agreeing that others are wrong to worry about it

Employers must stop
- Allowing any employee with a pattern of tardiness, sick leave, or other absence to continue unchecked

- Allowing the employee to work with dangerous equipment or to drive a company vehicle while under the influence

- Lightening the work load for an employee suspected of having a drinking problem; reassigning the employee to a less stressful position

- Excusing the employee's inappropriate behavior with coworkers or customers

- Pretending not to notice the smell of alcohol on the breath or the appearance of dilated/constricted pupils

- Keeping silent

Helping-professionals must stop

- Regarding the use of alcohol/drugs as a symptom of some other problem when it may already have developed into the primary disease of chemical dependence

- Trying to discover psycho-social causes of the alcohol/drug use before initiating intervention and treatment

- Making assessments and diagnoses solely according to the user's self-report; proceeding without enough objective information

- Focusing therapeutic efforts on "fixing" what happens as a result of using chemicals, rather than on the use of chemicals per se (for example, in marriage counseling, trying to prevent arguments by improving communication skills although most arguments start because one of the partners is drunk or high)

- Prescribing or recommending tranquilizers or other drugs to help the user cope with life

- Accepting excuses for missed and tardy appointments

- Allowing the user to enter a counseling session while under the influence of alcohol/drugs

- Continuing to counsel the user while the using keeps on; not requiring abstinence as a condition of treatment

- Trying to prevent feelings of guilt, when in fact it's appropriate for the user to feel guilty. Ordinarily it is *not* appropriate to say or imply, "Don't be too hard on yourself for breaking promises and letting your children down." Reassurance and consolation are forms of *enabling*. They take the user off the hook. The helping-professional should, instead, help the user take an honest look at the way other people are affected by the behavior. The professional must be there to help the user accept responsibility for those effects.

E. Systematic resistance

So far, in regard to the "dynamic tension" that can be used for effective intervention, we've considered **power**, **value conflicts**, **delusion and denial**, and **enabling**. All of these elements make themselves felt in a systematic resistance to change.

Many clinicians have written about the general pattern of relationships in families affected by chemical dependence. Family members tend to adopt specific roles and stay locked in these roles in order to cope. The self-concept of each member is in large part defined by the expectations of the rest of the family. All together the individuals become a self-perpetuating system.

Some of the roles assumed by family members are

- **The dutiful spouse.** Often assumes the role of caretaker or martyr.

- **The over-achieving child.** Helps convince other family members, especially the parents, that the family is normal and healthy despite some difficulties.

- **The rebellious child**. Tends to serve as a scapegoat, someone to blame for the family's problems.

- **The humorous/cute/attractive child.** Distracts the family from its problems by capturing attention when conflict is brewing.

- **The quiet, withdrawn child.** Avoids conflict by withdrawing into a private world. Unnoticed by the rest of the family, this child often gets lost in the struggle.

These roles may shift over time. Sometimes behavior changes quickly. The quiet, withdrawn child may start to rebel. The humorous/cute/attractive child may withdraw and fall silent. The high-achieving child may develop a serious behavioral disorder.

Family systems are highly resistant to change. One of the most crucial tasks of the professional is to help the family understand itself *as a system* so as to open itself enough to hear every member of the system and accept the changes required by the intervention.

When the chemically dependent person finally does accept help, the professional must continue with the family, helping them adjust to the changes—many of them difficult—that are bound to happen as the user stops using.

Take care not to exaggerate the possibilities!

Intervention cannot solve every problem. No matter how serious the chemical dependence seems to be, the helping-professional must never suggest that all the problems under discussion are caused by the use of alcohol/drugs. This is especially important if child abuse—or any other physical or emotional violence—has occurred. Although a chemically dependent person is usually more abusive when drinking/using than when sober, *the abuse may continue even after the using has stopped. The abuse itself will need to be addressed.*

It's unfair to allow the concerned persons to hope that all their burdens will be lighter if the user stops using. It is fair to tell them that most of their problems will continue until the using has stopped—because even if chemical dependence is not the cause of some problems, it certainly interferes with attempts to solve them.

CHAPTER 2

The Role of the Professional in Intervention

Introduction

Before any intervention is started, you must *identify the real client*.
As in most other contractual relationships, the client is whoever requested the service. Rarely will it be the one who is using alcohol/ drugs. Nearly always it will be someone concerned about the problem. *You are working for the concerned persons*, not for the user.

Why is this distinction important? Because you must remember to focus on the concerned persons, getting them ready to intervene and facilitating their session with the user. Through careful planning they must be prepared to express themselves effectively, use their power appropriately, and make their own decisions about their lives. Knowing they have done everything they can to help the user, they'll finally be able to let go.

When a chemically dependent person is already your client

It's not uncommon to discover the possibility of chemical dependence during counseling or therapy for something else. You may pick up cues that the use of chemicals is a problem affecting your client and the client's family and coworkers.

If the client's self-report about the use of alcohol/ drugs seems guarded or incomplete, you can ask permission to talk with the family. If they disclose more evidence that the use of chemicals is a problem, you can ask those concerned to prepare lists or letters describing the effects of the drinking or other drug use and then facilitate a session in which they present their statements to your client. In other words, you can adapt *The six steps of an effective intervention* described in Chapter 1. But remember that *the user* is still your client. You are not relating to the family as you would if they were the ones who had come to you for counseling.

Talking with the family without your client's permission violates federal laws about confidentiality. It also invites confusion, mistrust, and possible conflict of interest. (If the counselor gets very involved with the family, who is the real client?) Instead, recommend that family members get help for themselves through a group such as Al-Anon or that they seek the services of another qualified professional who can facilitate a structured intervention.

You must be forthright in telling your client that you have made these recommendations, and you must continue to provide the confrontation, insight, and support the client needs in order to change. It may come to the point where you have to say there is no point in continuing unless the client gets help for chemical dependence. To prevent confusion and possible conflict of interest, that help would need to come from another qualified source.

What if *you* are a chemically dependent person in recovery?

Many professional facilitators have been the subject of intervention and have sought treatment for chemical dependence. It's not rare for them to run into a familiar client or user at a meeting of Alcoholics Anonymous, Narcotics Anonymous, or another Twelve-Step program. How should such an encounter be handled?

Just as other aspects of the facilitator's life are handled. The personal and the professional are kept separate. There must be no confusion of roles.

Who does the intervention?

Not the helping-professional. The concerned persons are the ones who intervene. They are the ones who can bring legitimate personal, financial, or legal power to bear on the problem. In other words,

- Spouses and living companions intervene

- Children intervene

- Other relatives intervene

- Friends intervene

- Coworkers and colleagues intervene

- Employers intervene

- Probation officers and others with the power of law intervene

The intervenors are the ones who deliver the information, express their concern, exercise their power, and decide what they will do if the user agrees (or refuses) to accept help. The professional is there as a facilitator, giving guidance and support to those who care enough about the user—and care enough about themselves—to engage in a thoughtfully planned intervention.

Going it alone

As described in Chapter 1, some useful work can be accomplished by concerned persons acting alone. By acquainting themselves with the various defenses they use and learning how to talk openly about their feelings in relation to the user, concerned persons can do much to begin a healthful intervention.

The Johnson Institute has books, workbooks, and videos that can help concerned persons prepare for an intervention. These materials are very useful whether or not the concerned persons have access to professional help. (See Appendix C, *Johnson Institute Resources for Programming.*)

Experience has shown, however, that intervention is most effective with the help of a qualified professional facilitator, or interventionist. During the intervention session—and even while planning—many concerned persons are so emotionally involved that they tend to lose focus if a professional is not there to clarify the task, maintain perspective, and facilitate communication.

One mission of the Johnson Institute is to train helping-professionals to become effective facilitators of the intervention process. The Institute provides Professional Intervention Training Seminars throughout the United States and in other countries.[1]

---

[1] For information about Johnson Institute Professional Intervention Training Seminars (and about other training), call toll-free: 1-800-231-5165.

The National Council on Alcoholism and Drug Dependence (NCADD) offers intervention training for concerned persons.[2]

Some membership organizations offer information on how to intervene with chemically dependent members of their profession; for example, with physicians, nurses, psychologists, social workers, educators, lawyers, firefighters, police officers, pilots, or member of the clergy.[3]

Dangers of the "super counselor syndrome"

Have you ever been tempted to take over an intervention? Helping-professionals are not immune to grandiose thoughts of using their charisma and expertise to save people. Some occasionally assume power not rightfully theirs. The concerned persons take a back seat as the professional tries to badger the user into treatment.

Such an aggressive approach is not genuine intervention. It's mere confrontation and exercise of willpower. It's shallow and it's lazy, a poor substitute for careful planning. It's also ineffective. Usually it backfires, to the regret of all.

The "super counselor" may, in fact, be an unrecovering codependent.[4] This problem must be resolved before the helping-professional can be an effective interventionist. (See *Characteristics of a codependent* in Chapter 3.)

---

[2] The National Council on Alcoholism and Drug Dependence (NCADD) can be reached at 12 West 21st Street, New York, NY 10010. Phone (212) 206-6770. Or call 1-800-654-HOPE.

[3] Address inquiries to the local, state, or national organization that represents the profession.

[4] See *The Codependent Professional* in *Diagnosing and Treating Codependence*, by Timmen L. Cermak, M.D. Minneapolis:Johnson Institute, 1986. The book is listed in Appendix C, *Johnson Institute Resources for Programming*. For more information, call the Institute toll-free: 1-800-231-5165.

The professional as facilitator

The *six steps of an effective intervention* are clear and simple (see Chapter 1). But this does not mean intervention is easy. Each step can be misunderstood or misapplied if a qualified professional is not giving guidance. As a professional interventionist, or facilitator, your responsibilities are to

A. Assess the situation

B. Educate the concerned persons about the disease of chemical dependence

C. Provide information about the intervention process and the available help

D. Prepare the concerned persons to do the intervention

E. Facilitate the structured intervention session

F. Help the concerned persons process the content of the session and make decisions about their future

A. Assessing the situation

To assess the big picture and the necessary details, you need to

1. Help clients make a *preliminary assessment* of the effects the alcohol/drug use is having on all concerned

2. Help clients (concerned persons) look at their own use of chemicals

3. Help clients determine where the value conflicts lie

4. Help clients identify their strengths and weaknesses (readiness) for intervention

5. Help clients understand the power/leverage involved

1. Help clients make a preliminary assessment of the effects the alcohol/drug use is having on all concerned.

Structured intervention, as we're describing it here, is a powerful tool for addressing serious problems caused by the progressive disease of chemical dependence. It is not designed to address the problems of people who have had a few embarrassing incidents under the influence of alcohol/drugs or who are drinking more than usual in response to recent stress such as the loss of a job or some other singular trouble that arises in the normal course of life. This is why the professional interventionist needs to know how likely it is that the person identified for intervention truly has a problem of chemical dependence.

Your first task is to encourage the concerned persons to provide specific information and to help them step back and consider what they have said. Although a diagnosis of chemical dependence cannot be made solely from the information provided by the concerned persons, their information is crucial to the diagnostic process.

In the field of chemical dependence it's axiomatic that if you want to find out what a person's use of chemicals is *really* like, you'll talk not only with that person. You'll talk also with the spouse or living companion and with other members of the household. If the person lives alone or has no close relatives, you'll talk with knowledgeable friends. (Remember that any discussion with family or friends must be done with the person's permission. It must also be free of leading questions. The purpose is not to put ideas into people's heads.) If your approach is empathetic and objective, and if you reach the people who really know what's going on, their comments will show whether there is a pattern of alcohol/drug use indicating a serious problem. For example, was the spouse of the "alcoholic" previously in a marriage that failed because of alcoholism? Do you perceive any hidden agenda?

If you're not sure of a concerned person's sincerity or credibility, you must settle that issue as quickly as possible. If, for example, you discover a child custody battle is looming between parents while one parent is preparing to intervene with the other, you must halt the intervention until the matter is cleared up. (In that example, the concerned person is also a legal adversary, creating a probable conflict of interest.) You need to decide how legitimate and healthful an intervention would be and when it should proceed—if it should proceed at all.

What information are you seeking from the concerned persons? You need to know not only the *effects* of the alcohol/drug use on self and others, but also to what extent the user manifests *warning signs* of chemical dependence:

Ten Warning Signs of Chemical Dependence

1. Preoccupation. Does the person look forward to the next drink/pill/fix? Is the day often planned around getting the chemical or trying to avoid it? Does the person find reasons/excuses to drink or use? Does the person become irritable or agitated if unable to drink/use at certain times, such as after work, before dinner, or at social functions where no alcohol is served? Does conversation often turn to drinking or getting high?

2. Increased tolerance. Does it now take more alcohol/drugs to get drunk or high than it used to?

3. Medicinal drinking/drug use. Does the person self-medicate with alcohol/drugs to dull physical or emotional pain or to cope with feelings of sadness, anger, fear, and even joy? Does the person use chemicals to bolster courage? Does the person use chemicals as a quick pick-me-up to overcome fatigue?

4. Blackouts. Has the person ever had blackouts? How many? How often? (See *Blackouts* in Chapter 1.)

5. Gulping drinks; rushing the high. Does the person take a few quick belts to get that euphoric or cozy feeling as fast as possible? Does the person drink directly from the bottle? Does the person drink/use before a party, to get a head start on the celebration?

6. Using more than intended. Does the person plan to take just a drink or two but end up getting drunk? Does the person often stop at a bar for a quick drink after work and stay until closing time?

7. Using alone. Does the person drink/use in private, with the goal of getting drunk or high?

8. Using at inappropriate times or places. Does the person drink/use in the morning or early afternoon? Does the person drink/use on the job or at other inappropriate times or places?

9. Hiding supplies. Does the person keep liquor or other drugs in secret places, planning to drink or use without detection?

10. Defensiveness. Does the person become hostile or defensive when questioned about drinking/using?

For the preliminary assessment a professional can also use more formal tools, such as the *Substance Abuse Subtle Screening Inventory (SASSI)*. The advantage of the SASSI is that it's very well standardized and its items are not transparent.

The brief *Michigan Alcohol Screening Test (MAST)* may be too transparent if administered only to the person whose drinking is at issue. The person may find it easy to shade answers. The MAST is most useful when administered to both the problem drinker and the spouse or living companion.

The *Children of Alcoholics Screening Test (CAST)* is a 30-item instrument that addresses the difficulties children may have in living with a problem drinker. It's used not only to help children identify the problems they're experiencing, but also to confront the drinker with facts about the ways in which alcohol is affecting family life. The children's test responses can be very persuasive in convincing a problem drinker to face the facts and accept help.

Remember that the screening and other information-gathering activities for a preliminary assessment are not sufficient for diagnosis, and so they do not qualify for third-party reimbursement. Preliminary assessments are often conducted within an hour at an HMO or other clinic. When a client is referred for treatment after a quick assessment, professionals in the treatment program must act swiftly to gather more data for an accurate diagnosis.

2. Help clients (concerned persons) look at their own use of chemicals.

Some clients who approach you because of concern for a loved one may themselves be chemically dependent. You need to explore the possibility. If you think a client may be chemically dependent but not in recovery, that issue must be clarified before intervention is started. Occasionally a concerned person and an apparent user (such as a wife and a husband) may *both* need treatment for chemical dependence.

Not all users are in the same stage of dependence on alcohol/drugs. A woman with a drinking problem, for example, may seek help for her alcoholic husband, who has frequent blackouts and occasional seizures or delirium tremens. In such a case you would focus on the husband, whose drinking problem is more severe than his wife's. If he accepts treatment, she will probably have to be involved. This requirement may serve as a catalyst to get the wife to recognize and accept treatment for her own chemical dependence. (On the other hand, it may be necessary to exclude the wife from the intervention, lest the identified alcoholic switch the focus to her.)

3. Help clients (concerned persons) determine where the value conflicts lie.

To decide what kind of leverage (internal or external)— and how much leverage—will be needed to conduct a successful intervention, you need to know how guilty or conflicted the chemically dependent person feels about causing trouble and unhappiness for other people.

If the user has a history of immature, irresponsible acting-out (such as leaving the house abruptly when confronted about being intoxicated), the intervention is likely to fail unless it involves *external* leverage; for example, the economic power of an employer. If the user has a history of sociopathic behavior or law-breaking, the intervention is likely to fail unless the *external* legal power of a judge or probation officer can be used. If the user cares not at all about the concerned persons or about hurting other people, the kind of intervention described in this book will not be effective and therefore should not be attempted.

(See also #5 below, *Help clients understand the power/leverage involved*.)

4. Help clients identify their strengths and weaknesses (readiness) for intervention.

The professional has to make a decision about each concerned person's *ability to recognize problems* stemming from chemical dependence and *ability to follow through* on tasks required for successful intervention. Reality requires that the concerned persons understand their own readiness for intervention. This includes an ability to recognize their fears.

If a person close to the user is deeply deluded about the seriousness of the problem and cannot understand how enabling works, it will be necessary for that person (who may be codependent) to engage in therapy, counseling, a self-help group, or a support group to acquire enough insight and strength to participate in a structured intervention. (See *The concerned persons group* in Chapter 3.)

5. Help clients understand the power/leverage involved.

To intervene successfully, the concerned persons need to know what power the user has and what power they have as individuals and as a group. By defining the kinds and strength of power each person possesses, the relative weaknesses or lack of power will also be revealed.

To help participants recognize the power/leverage they can use—and the power/leverage that can be used against them—you must determine:

- What matters to the user? What does the user value most? Specifically, how much does the user care about each concerned person? How much does the user care about staying in a marriage or other close relationship? How much does the user care about each child involved? How much does the user care about coworkers? How much does the user care about work or career? How important is personal reputation? What kinds of loss would cause this person great sadness or fear?

- How emotionally dependent on the user is each concerned person? How financially dependent does each concerned person feel? How realistic are these feelings of dependence? What does the user do to reinforce the person's feelings of emotional and/or financial dependence? What risk is each person willing to take in regard to emotional dependence? What risk in regard to financial dependence?

- What persuasive legal issues can the concerned persons present, such as facts about probation, parole, and court-ordered commitment?

- As a group, are the concerned persons powerful enough? Will they need external leverage from someone close to the user but not in the group? Will they need any additional power of law?

Besides helping concerned persons identify their power, the professional must help them understand how to use it appropriately. The professional must also help them understand how to keep any feelings of dependence or other weakness from undermining their use of legitimate leverage. Many people—especially senior adults—are reluctant to acknowledge and use the leverage they have. Brief assertiveness training usually works well in preparing them to embrace their power and use it effectively.

B. Educating the concerned persons about the disease of chemical dependence

So far, you've been assessing the situation to gain a view of the big picture and the necessary details. In the process you have also been guiding your clients 1) to make a preliminary assessment of the effects the alcohol/drug use is having on all concerned, 2) to look at their own use of chemicals, 3) to determine where the value conflicts lie, 4) to identify their strengths and weaknesses (readiness) for intervention, and 5) to understand the power/leverage involved.

Although their preliminary assessment will not be definitive—and even a professional interventionist cannot make a definitive diagnosis without meeting directly with the user—sometimes the evidence provided by the concerned persons is so overwhelming that there's no question of chemical dependence. When, for example, a wife reports that her husband has had four DWIs in the past two years, has been drunk every weekend for the past five years, has been hiding liquor for the past 15 years, and has been to Alcoholics Anonymous several times but dropped out—and when the wife is credible and does not contradict herself—it's obvious that alcoholism is a problem for this family.

The concerned persons may not see it this way, however. They may think they are the cause of the pain. They may think that if they can change whatever is wrong with themselves, the alcoholic will no longer be driven to drink. They may blame the use of chemicals on job stress or believe it's a bad habit the user can stop by mustering up the willpower to "just say no."

Such mistaken notions will not be corrected simply by gathering more observations or describing more feelings. What the concerned persons need is *knowledge* about chemical dependence and what can be done about it.

What all concerned persons need to know

It's up to the helping-professional to educate all concerned persons (not only those who express mistaken notions) about

- The disease of chemical dependence and how the disease progresses

- How the disease affects the lives of those who are closest to the user

- How delusion, denial, and enabling encourage the disease to get worse

- The basic principles of intervention

In education sessions, the professional separates fiction from facts about chemical dependence. The information frees clients to change their attitudes and behavior toward the user (attitudes and behavior that have only reinforced the problem). The education about chemical dependence is not finished when the principles of intervention are covered. It continues well into the process of recovery, supporting the concerned persons as changes take place.

Why treat chemical dependence as a disease?

In 1956 the American Medical Association (AMA) defined alcoholism—and, by extension, other drug dependence—as a disease; in other words, as a deviation from a state of health, with a describable train of symptoms. Whether or not you agree that chemical dependence is a disease, keep in mind the benefits this approach can bring to intervention:

- It takes chemical dependence out of the realm of morality. No longer is it a matter of moral weakness and lack of willpower. It's a matter of disease—an insidious disease that sneaks up on a person and takes hold without the person's awareness. Because no one deliberately falls victim to it, chemically dependent people are not to be condemned, demeaned, or looked down upon. Do not underestimate how important this moral/medical distinction can be for both the users and the concerned persons. When chemical dependence is equated with moral weakness and lack of willpower, the shame keeps sufferers from seeking help.

- It assures family members that they are not the cause of the problem. (You may be surprised to learn how many do hold themselves responsible for a loved one's use of alcohol or other drugs.) Parents, siblings, spouses, and children of alcoholics and other drug-dependent people can understand that they have not caused this progressive disease.

- Concerned persons, and often the users themselves, are heartened when they find out there are treatment facilities and many other services available for people affected by the disease of chemical dependence. When users are labeled as morally weak or lacking willpower, they're left with virtually no place to turn.

- Many researchers have concluded that genetics plays a major role in some types of alcoholism.

It's not necessary to give clients the history of the disease concept or to explain whether the user meets every criterion established for the diagnosis of disease. What's important is that concerned persons learn to recognize and accept the problem realistically. This is made easier by knowing that for decades, millions of other people have experienced, recognized, accepted, and successfully dealt with the same problem.

Family members, especially, need to know *they are not alone*. This knowledge helps them let go of the guilt and shame that have kept them stuck in their pain. Along with new insights about relevant family issues, the knowledge that they're not alone breaks down the isolation of family members and sustains their hope that things will change.

An abundance of information

There are many resources for learning about chemical dependence, including books and videos illustrating delusion and denial and the ways enablers contribute to the problem. (See Appendix C, *Johnson Institute Resources for Programming.*)

Vernon E. Johnson's easy-to-read book *Intervention: How to Help Someone Who Doesn't Want Help* gives concerned persons a clear, succinct overview of chemical dependence and the intervention process. For intervention with adolescents, an especially useful book is *Choices & Consequences: What to Do When a Teenager Uses Alcohol/Drugs. A Step-by-Step System That Really Works*, by Dick Schaefer.

The video series *Back to Reality: What We Need to Know to Conquer Addiction* shows how chemical dependence develops and how it affects the user's family, friends, and coworkers. It also dramatizes the dynamics of enabling and shows how a structured intervention works.

C. Providing information about the intervention process and the available help

People who are locked into a pattern of behavior governed by chemical dependence in their families—or in their workplace or circle of friends—are often discouraged. Knowing that efforts to help the user have failed in the past, or that the user has quit Alcoholics Anonymous, or that time spent in jail for drunk driving has made no difference, they think little can be done to improve the situation because "nothing has worked."

Those who feel discouraged and doubtful need to know that the process of structured intervention, followed by treatment, is designed for the problem they're facing—and that it works. They need to know that many people before them have tried one-on-one interventions and single-session interventions without success, but that others who have engaged in structured intervention followed by a treatment program and aftercare have seen amazing changes in their lives.

Make sure the information is specific.

Specific instructions reduce anxiety and increase the likelihood that clients will follow through with the entire intervention process.

Besides general information about the content and effectiveness of services available, clients need to know exactly *whom to reach for treatment, how to reach them, and what to say*. If you don't specify names for referral, anxious clients are likely to start telling their life stories to the switchboard operator. Tell the person who will be making arrangements what number to call, what person or service to ask for, what information to provide, and how to handle possible difficulties. If, for example, a bed is necessary but not available, the caller should be prepared to ask when one will be available, how it can be reserved, and how the caller will be told it's ready.

If the provider is an HMO or other clinic operating under managed care, or if health insurance restrictions apply, clients should be told what to expect. Traditional treatment in a residential facility is not the only effective way to help the chemically dependent person. (See *Why make treatment the major focus of intervention?* and *What are the qualities of an excellent treatment program?* in Chapter 4.)

Be ready to to make most of the arrangements yourself. Some service providers don't recognize a family member as the proper one to make contact for admission. They require a professional's referral. You need to know the procedure at each facility so as not to send the client off on a fruitless mission.

D. Preparing the concerned persons to do the intervention

The concerned persons, especially family members, may need considerable counseling and support as they prepare for the structured intervention with the user. Some may be ready within a day. Others may be so fearful or dysfunctional that they'll not be ready for months—in which case the professional and the other concerned persons (preferably in consultation with the fearful/ dysfunctional members) will need to decide whether to go ahead without them. Still others may have to be excluded because they themselves are chemically dependent and not in recovery. (Yet keep in mind that some current users can, with guidance from the facilitator, be effective intervenors.) If the group decides to wait, they'll need to decide how long. You will have to decide whether to provide the necessary counseling yourself, or whether to recommend other appropriate resources, including Al-Anon, for anyone not ready to participate.

Al-Anon[5] should be recommended to all close relatives and friends of chemically dependent persons, especially those who may become intervenors and those who have participated in an intervention. Not all Al-Anon groups are alike, however, and so clients should be given guidance as they go about choosing a group. They should be encouraged to try more than one and to find someone, such as a good Al-Anon sponsor, to help them process their experiences. They should also be made aware that Al-Anon is not a place to seek help for the user; it's a place to get help for themselves. It's a fellowship of persons who are dedicated to each other's mental, emotional, and spiritual growth.

---

[5] What is said here about Al-Anon applies also to Alateen, Adult Children of Alcoholics, or any similar group that employs the principles of Alcoholics Anonymous—most essentially the Twelve Steps.

Structuring the intervention

As the one who facilitates the planning and confrontation, you have five major tasks:

1. Helping your clients decide who will participate; then helping to get those people involved

2. Helping concerned persons prepare the information they'll present to the user

3. Making sure a treatment program is selected and ready; arranging insurance coverage

4. Guiding the concerned persons through an intervention rehearsal

5. Deciding where and when to hold the intervention and what to tell the user beforehand

1. Helping your clients decide who will participate; then helping to get those people involved. The concerned persons must decide who among them are so meaningful to the user that their participation will increase the likelihood of success.

   Who should be selected, and why? With your clients, consider these guidelines:
   - People directly affected by the user's behavior—usually family members, close friends, and close coworkers—have credibility and personal/emotional power, or leverage, with the user.

   - Relatives outside the immediate family are often in a position to observe the effects on the family, because they're not caught up in the delusion and denial that affect those living in the household. Caring aunts, uncles, and grandparents have frequently played a major role in presenting information, then supporting other concerned persons in their observations and helping the user to hear and accept what is said.

- Employers, supervisors, probation officers, family physicians, clergy, and others with external power can exert personal, financial, occupational, or legal leverage to get the user to accept help.

- Anyone the user loves, likes, respects, feels close to, or feels dependent on should be considered for selection if they have first-hand knowledge of the problem.

Have clients compose a list of meaningful concerned persons. Then review the list with them. Is it complete? Have any key people been omitted? If so, why? Might these people sabotage the process if they're not included in the intervention and in the important educational process that goes with it? If sabotage is possible, what should be done to prevent it or counteract it?

What should be done if a person on the list is too fearful or dysfunctional to go ahead with intervention? What if someone is chemically dependent but not yet in treatment? Should you put off the intervention? If so, for how long? (Keep in mind that some chemically dependent persons who still use alcohol/drugs can participate effectively. Whether or not to include them requires careful judgment by the clients, guided by the professional.)

What about geographic distance? How much time can the nonlocal people spend away from home? What about transportation? To unite participants from various parts of the state or country, the face-to-face intervention planning and confrontation will have to be accomplished in one to three days. (Even with unlimited time it makes no sense to have the activity take weeks. And insurance plans and managed-care facilities do not allow so much time.) Even more important: How interested are the nonlocal people in helping the user? Why do the nonlocal people care about recovery?

NCADD's National Intervention Network can provide information to help with widely scattered families.[6]

Asking those selected to intervene

It's not easy to gather meaningful persons for intervention. Even if they all live close by, and even if each one cares deeply about the user, they tend to back off when another concerned person invites them to help confront the problem. You, as a professional with a structured program, are in a much better position to rally forces. A worried family member or friend need not ask people to intervene—just ask them to attend one meeting to talk with a counselor. That's all. You take it from there.

Having a professional explain the importance of intervention and its record of success may be enough to get listeners involved. Their word-of-mouth recommendations may persuade others to join them.

2. Helping concerned persons prepare the information they'll present to the user. The user must be confronted with clients' specific observations and feelings about

- *Harmful incidents caused by the use of alcohol/drugs:* Not only instances of physical injury and danger, but also instances of emotional and social injury and jeopardy, such as fear, hurt feelings, embarrassment, shunning/ostracism, and degradation

---

[6] See the address and telephone number in footnote #2

- *Changes in chemical use over time:* How the intake has increased; how it has become faster and more frequent; how the user can no longer stop; how chemicals are hidden; how the person uses at inappropriate times and places; and so forth (See *Ten Warning Signs of Chemical Dependence* earlier in this chapter.)

- *Changes in health and behavior over the years:* For example, loss of appetite; weight loss or gain; gastrointestinal problems; sedentariness; loss of strength; loss of interest in appearance; neglect of home; impotency or impaired sexual performance; frequent insomnia; blackouts; frequent tardiness or absence from work because of binges or hangovers; diminished productivity; financial irresponsibility; loss of drive and ambition; loss of interest in leisure activities; child abuse or neglect; elder abuse or neglect

All incidents and changes must have been witnessed by the person presenting them. Second-hand reports won't do. Nothing may be gossip or hearsay. Examples must be specific. ("I remember the time you hit my mom in the stomach and I was scared she was going to die.")

Regarding changes in health and behavior: A simple, general statement of concern can be very effective if it comes from a credible, meaningful person after others have presented their specific observations.

How to extract all the information you can and make it usable

- *Clearly describe each incident.* Exactly what did the person do under the influence of alcohol/drugs? What led to what? What was the date and time? How did the person look and sound? Who else was there? How did the onlookers react?

- *Connect each incident directly to the use of alcohol/drugs.*

- *State your feelings about each incident. Exactly how were you affected?*

> Troy, last Friday when you came home, it was 2:00 A.M. and you had a can of beer in your hand. You said you'd gone to Pete's Bar after work. I didn't know where you were. I thought you might have been hurt or killed. I was worried sick.
>
> Tasha, when you wrecked the car I thought you were going to die. I was scared and angry at the same time. We both used to brag what a good driver you were. It's frightening to see what happens when you drink.
>
> Dad, when I was a little kid, you would leave me in the car outside the bar for hours. I didn't know what to do. I'd be bored and scared. I was afraid that somebody would break into the car and that you might not come back. I can still see you walking away, and it still leaves me feeling abandoned.
>
> Donna, when the children need you and I need you, you're out with your friends using cocaine. It hurts when you skip out on us like that. I didn't know what to say last week when little Jesse said your friends are more important than we are.
>
> Jamie, last Saturday you said you'd help me with my car. I waited and waited, but

you never did show up, and you didn't answer your phone. I was disappointed and more than a little annoyed when I realized the car wouldn't be ready to drive to work. When I finally got in touch with you on Sunday, you said you had stopped for a beer and that helping with the car just slipped your mind. This isn't the first time you've done this. It hurts my feelings when you put drinking ahead of me.

Casey, when you called me at work on Monday, you were slurring your words. Your voice got louder and louder, and you kept repeating yourself. The guy next to me could even hear it. The whole scene was so upsetting that I went into the bathroom to compose myself. I was shaking like a leaf. Then I had to go back and face everybody. I dread getting another phone call like that.

Miguel, last year you drank all during *Cinco de Mayo*. Then you got sick all over the floor. At first I got scared because I thought it was a heart attack. When I realized you weren't sick—you were drunk—I felt embarrassed and angry. I love you very much. But I still feel angry about what your drinking is doing to us as a family and to you as a person.

Mom, I don't bring friends home anymore because I never know if you'll be drunk or sober. When I brought Vince home on the last day of school, you screamed and swore at us. Vince won't come back here again. I hate how your mood changes when you drink. You're not yourself. And I dread being humiliated in front of my friends.

Joan, we've been friends for a long time, and so I trust you'll hear me out on this. At the party the other night I saw you take a couple of tranquilizers and then you had a least four drinks. You said some terrible things to my boyfriend that hurt his feelings. You wouldn't have done that if you'd been sober. I feel as if I'm losing you as a friend. And if you keep taking pills and drinking like that, I'm afraid you'll die and I'll really lose you.

Be sure to write lists!

During the planning phase, everyone in the group needs to make a list of what to say to the user. (Some professionals prefer that letters be read. Lists should be prepared before the letters are written.) The lists or letters will be taken to the intervention session and held plainly in sight as they're read aloud by the people who wrote them. (See the second of *The six steps of an effective intervention* in Chapter 1.)

Why are written lists important?

- They make it possible for the facilitator to weed out vague, accusatory, or demeaning statements before the confrontation

- They strengthen the concerned persons' commitment to the intervention

- They keep the concerned persons clearly focused on what they are there for

- They help the concerned persons remember what to say

- They show the user how much caring, commitment, and time the concerned persons have invested in the hope of change

- They show that the concerned persons are organized and goal-directed

- They help keep the user from interrupting

What about confidential information?

It's unethical, and even illegal, for the helping-professional to gather data from employers, doctors, and others if the one who is the subject of intervention has not signed releases of confidential data. Also it's important to assure the family that you will seek the user's permission before trying to gather such data. (If the user is a minor, you need to seek permission of a parent or other legal guardian.)

Because it can be more therapeutic for *family members* to collect the information and learn how to ask relevant questions, the helping-professional should not forge ahead without a compelling reason that the family members should not be required to collect the information themselves. Some of it might already be on hand. A wife, for example, might have legitimate access to employment information and medical records in files at home, where her alcoholic husband has already seen them.

3. Making sure a treatment program is selected and ready; arranging insurance coverage. You'll find that most alcoholics/addicts have tried, or been urged to try, other paths to sobriety—without success. They may have tried to cut down on their drinking/drug use. They may have tried to quit by themselves. They may have attended meetings of Alcoholics Anonymous, Cocaine Anonymous, or Narcotics Anonymous. They may have gone back on promises to stop acting up at parties. Generally it's best if futile efforts *have* been made before a structured intervention is arranged. These failures make it easier for the group—including the user—to agree on the need for qualified professional help.

Choosing a treatment program

You must locate an effective treatment program *before* embarking on the intervention. But how can you find a qualified program? How can you distinguish an excellent program from one that is poor or mediocre? Before you refer anyone to a treatment program, you may need to visit the facility to see how the program actually works.[7]

A good treatment program—

- Will have a qualified, licensed staff of Certified Chemical Dependence Specialists[8]

- Will devote sufficient time to evaluation, so that staff can determine with certainty whether the problem of alcohol/drug use is actually chemical dependence

- Will conduct an evaluation that's intense and powerful, so that the sheer amount of information gained, along with keen observations by other patients and the guidance of experienced and professional staff, will break through the defenses that remain after the structured intervention and will convince the user to complete the program

- Will integrate the philosophy and steps of Alcoholics Anonymous

---

[7] If your search has not been fruitful, call the Johnson Institute toll-free: 1-800-231-5165. Be ready to describe what you need.

[8] See Appendix B, *Johnson Institute Standards for Professional Interventionists*.

- Will have a clearly defined family counseling program to parallel the program for the patient; preferably a program that includes close friends as well[9]

- Will have an aftercare program not only for the patient, but also for family members and for the close friends who wish to carry through

- Will, compared with other programs, have a high percentage of clients (people who have gone through treatment) still recovering—rather than using again—after one year, two years, five years, ten years

The treatment program must be ready to accept the user the moment the session is over. And the concerned persons must be ready for the user's objections:

But we're right in the middle of a major contract proposal!

That's not a problem. We already have that covered with Kim and Mario.

I can't possibly take time away from home! Who will get the kids off to school?

Don't worry. I've talked with my boss, and I'll be going to work a half hour later so I can take care of the kids.

But my classes! What's going to happen to my students?

That's all taken care of. Sarah will be taking your English classes, and I'll be working with your creative writing club.

---

[9] It's highly appropriate to have a program including close friends, especially if the user has no family.

If a managed care facility will not cooperate with coverage—at least for a formal assessment in a treatment center—don't hesitate to use your state insurance commissioner for leverage.

The transition to treatment

It's more than a matter of professional courtesy to inform the treatment program admissions counselor about 1) the circumstances leading to the intervention, 2) who was involved, 3) the feeling-level responses of the user, the family members, and other concerned persons, and 4) what the treatment program staff can expect upon the patient's arrival. The success of the treatment program will depend partly on your communication with treatment staff.

During the post-intervention session, the concerned persons have a chance to process their feelings with the facilitator and achieve a degree of resolution. (See *Helping the concerned persons process the content of the session and make decisions about their future*, later in this chapter.) But the user rarely has this opportunity. Often a user arrives at a treatment program with rising emotions of anger, resentment, fear, guilt, and shame. If the program fails to provide a chance to process these feelings with a capable and sensitive counselor before evaluation and treatment begin, the feelings can seriously interfere with progress and impede recovery.

In other words, some treatment programs are unprepared for the intense emotions of a patient who has just been the subject of a structured intervention. You can help. In your planning for intervention, include a plan for follow-through with treatment staff.

Why a primary treatment program? Why not Alcoholics Anonymous?

Why make treatment the major focus of intervention? If most users attend A.A. or a similar program after treatment, why not save time and money by going there directly from intervention?

The issue is not whether A.A. is more or less effective than a treatment program. A.A. is very effective *for those who remain in the fellowship*. Receiving primary treatment before entering A.A. (or a similar Twelve-Step program for other drug use) will, we believe, increase the probability that the chemically dependent person will stay in the fellowship and fully recover.

What about "what if" clauses?

The video *I'll Quit Tomorrow* portrays an intervention with an alcoholic who promises to stay sober on his own instead of going to treatment. The family decides to go along with this as long as he accepts the "what if" clause: *What if you don't stay sober?* He agrees to go to treatment if he takes another drink.

Some helping-professionals think a "what if" has no place in intervention because it lets the user escape the pressure of the moment. Indeed it does, and for that reason a "what if" should not be presented or accepted as an alternative to treatment unless it's the only action the user is willing to take. That possibility is one of the contingencies that must be covered when you and the concerned persons make plans for intervention. Will a "what if" clause be allowed, or not? Under exactly what conditions? (See step 3 of *The six steps of an effective intervention* in Chapter 1.)

4. Guiding the concerned persons through an intervention rehearsal. The intervention session will be smoother and more effective if you and the intervenors have rehearsed it. Follow these steps:

    A. Choose and prepare a leader

    B. Decide the order in which group members will speak

    C. Decide on seating arrangements

    D. Role-play the introduction, presentation, and conclusion

    E. Clarify what each concerned person will do if the user rejects every alternative

A. Choose and prepare a leader

Someone other than the user's spouse or living companion should be chosen to speak for the group. Ordinarily there are too many conflicting emotions between partners. You don't want the user to infer that everything is being orchestrated by the partner.

The group dynamics will be most effective if the leader is someone the user already knows and respects and finds credible, such as a trusted friend. You can assist as needed.

Make sure the leader knows how to start and how to finish. This requires a person who can

- *Express care and concern.* The leader sets the tone of compassion and respect by explaining that everyone is there because they care about the person, are concerned about the person, and want to talk about those concerns.

- **Get the user to agree not to respond until all the concerned persons have finished speaking.** This ground rule is crucial. If the leader allows the user to interrupt or to respond prematurely, the cumulative effect of the information and feelings expressed will be dissipated. The rule should be presented in a gentle manner:

  > I know you'll want to respond to what you hear. But I'm asking you to agree to let everyone say what they have to say first. I promise you'll have time to respond. Will you agree to that?

- **Tell the user exactly what the group wants him or her to do.** After all those concerned have finished their statements, the leader begins with a love statement (to reduce defenses) and then states exactly what the group wants the person to do. Each speaker will already have expressed the desire that the user get help, but *the specific nature of that help is left until the end:*

  > Bill, we have an interview set up with a counselor at Avonridge, and a bed is ready for you. We've done this because we want you back in our lives healthy and sober.

Notice that the statement is brief and firm but considerate. It ends with the uplifting goal. At this point, the leader asks whether the person is willing to go now. If the answer is yes: It's time to hug and get moving.

If the answer is no: Give the user time to respond. Now the leader will prevent the concerned persons from interrupting. It's at this point that the leader, backed by you and the rest of the group, must be ready to accept or reject a "what if" clause.

B. Decide the order in which group members will speak

Have the group give careful thought to the sequence of speakers. Build up to a finale. As a general rule, the immediate family members—especially the children—should speak *after* those outside the family unit have spoken. The later, powerful statements from close family members are often the ones that convince the user to accept treatment. Some facilitators recommend that the children or the boss speak last.

Be aware that the first speakers can reinforce or ruin the caring, respectful atmosphere you have tried to establish. Select those who can help break the ice and promote listening without interruption.

C. Decide on seating arrangements

Like the sequence of speakers, you need to plan the order of seating. The leader must be ready to show everyone where to sit.

- Don't seat the user near the door. In that location it's too easy to walk out.

- Do seat the user across the room. Put concerned persons in front of the door. Create a psychological barrier across the exit.

- Don't seat the spouse or living companion next to the user. It tempts the user to distract the group and to focus anger and fear on the partner.

- Do seat a calm, close friend next to the user— perhaps the person who escorted the user to the meeting.

D. Role-play the introduction, presentation, and conclusion

Before the rehearsal, the leader arranges the seating and chooses a nonfamily member to play the role of the user.

As the intervenors enter the room, the leader directs them to their chairs. If refreshments are served before the session, they're to be finished and discarded before intervenors are seated.

In your role as the professional, you greet the seated intervenors. You then instruct them not to drink any alcohol before the actual intervention session because the odor is distracting. You also tell them not to laugh, joke, chew gum, smoke, drink a beverage, drum their fingers, roll their eyes, exchange glances, or in any other way distract the user or each other during the session. The session must be treated with seriousness and dignity. Everyone must listen carefully. The atmosphere must convey love, respect, and genuine concern.

The chemically dependent person is brought in by the escort and seated as planned.

The leader turns to the person, expressing care and concern:

> Terry, I know you're surprised to see us all here today, and I can imagine it feels uncomfortable too. We're here because you're very important to us. We all love you, and we're concerned about you. We want to talk about our concerns.

The leader explains that *independent statements* will be read by the concerned persons, expressing their personal observations and feelings.

The leader gets the user to agree not to interrupt, and gives assurance that there will be time to respond when everyone has finished.

Group members then follow the planned sequence in reading their lists or letters. They address the user, not each other or the leader or the facilitator. As each presentation is finished, it's critiqued by the group, before the next presentation is started. (You can check each one against guidelines in *Helping concerned persons prepare the information they'll present to the user*, earlier in this chapter.) The group makes sure that every presentation

- Expresses compassion

- Avoids an angry, accusatory tone

- Describes both factual observations and personal feelings

- Ties observations and feelings directly to the use of alcohol/drugs

- States only first-hand experiences, not gossip or second-hand information

- Avoids asking questions, because questions invite answers and arguments, interrupting the flow and diluting the cumulative effect

- Concludes with a statement of what the presenter wants. ("I want us all to get help." "I want my dad back.")

This all builds up to the finale, when leader turns to the user, makes a love statement, states exactly what the group recommends be done, and asks whether the user will do what is asked.

The user's response

It's normal for the user to challenge the concerned persons about labels. ("Are you saying I'm an alcoholic?" "Are you calling me a drug addict?") If a diagnosis has not been confirmed—for example, in a previous treatment program—the leader or another intervenor responds with a label-free message such as,

> We do know that your drinking [drug use] has been hurting all of us. In fact, your use of alcohol [drugs] is causing some very difficult problems. We want us all to get help. Each one of us will take a look at our own part in this. We're asking you to join us by going in for an evaluation. The first part of your time there will be devoted to evaluation. We want us all to get help, and this is the beginning.

(See also *Listen for surrender words* in *Facilitating the intervention session,* later in this chapter.)

What if emotions begin to take over?

At the start of the intervention process, many concerned persons feel overwhelmed by their anger. While role-playing they might express rage, resentment, opinions, and blame. If this happens in your group, explain how destructive these expressions would be in the actual session. Help them talk through their feelings with you and the other participants. You might have them role-play their raw feelings as another concerned person temporarily takes over the role of the user. Help them understand that beneath the anger are *feelings of hurt and disappointment*. Make sure they know that these are the feelings to express—not the resulting anger. Then have them role-play the appropriate communication to see what a difference it makes. If a very angry person is still unwilling or unable to express feelings appropriately, refer to the contingency plan you've worked out with the group. Either delay the intervention session or proceed without that member. (See *Who should be selected, and why?* earlier in this chapter.)

E. Clarify what each concerned person will do if the user rejects every alternative

This is where power and leverage come into play. Remind the intervenors of their emotional, economic, and/or legal power as it affects the user. Help them decide what power they are willing to use. For example, if the husband of an alcoholic feels he can no longer tolerate his home life and will leave if his wife continues to drink, he must be willing to say so and stand by that statement. If an employer decides she will have to fire a drug user if his performance continues to be poor, the employer must be clear about it and not allow anyone to persuade her otherwise.

This is no time for bluffing, hesitating, or backing down. Even if the user refuses treatment now, it may well be accepted at a later session if the intervenors have been steadfast and consistent. When intervenors undermine their own credibility, they give the user leverage for resisting—and almost guarantee that a later intervention will fail.

Because so much depends on the credibility of every concerned person, the facilitator must take care not to prompt participants to say something they don't really mean or commit to something they can't or won't really do.

Another word of caution: Although the concerned persons must decide what they will do if the user rejects every alternative, intervention is not a matter of winning or losing. *Effective intervention is not a power struggle.* It is not a contest. It is a respectful and caring presentation of the reality that all participants must face, and of the options available to them. The atmosphere of respect must be maintained. If it's momentarily lost, you as the professional facilitator must step in and restore it. You can, for example, tell the group that everyone is to be complimented for giving it their all.

5. Deciding where and when to hold the intervention and what to tell the user beforehand. The session should be held on neutral ground where the seating arrangement can be controlled—not in the user's home, where the person can turn on the television, walk away, or order the group to leave. At a neutral location, the power and safety of the home turf cannot come into play.

A conference room in the professional's office building would be appropriate. The family physician's office would also be appropriate. A lawyer's office or a room at the user's place of employment may or may not be perceived as neutral.

The time should not be delayed just because it's inconvenient for some participants. It should be as soon as proper preparation allows. Those who absolutely cannot attend may send videotapes or audiotapes.

Bringing the user to the site

The group decides who will bring the user to the intervention session. Usually a spouse or other partner or relative tells the user that they have an appointment to talk with a counselor about their family problems or about problems in their relationship. This is not subterfuge; it's an honest statement. An employer who brings an employee might reveal more of the subject. ("There are problems on the project that need to be cleared up. One thing I'm concerned about is how drinking/drug use may be getting in the way.")

The user may be overwhelmed and frightened away by the prospect of facing even a few people. If pinned down about the purpose of the meeting and who else will be there, the escort should use her or his own judgment about how specific to be. (See *Is surprise really important? Is it right?* in Chapter 4.)

The leader addresses the confusion when the session starts:

> Pat, I know you must be surprised to see us all here. We decided to have a meeting because everyone in this room cares about you and is worried about you.

The user will be surprised, and perhaps angry, to see the waiting group. However, the expression of care, concern, and love is disarming. Usually it gets everyone through that initial, awkward phase of the intervention session.

E. Facilitating the intervention session

All concerned persons except the one bringing the user to the meeting should arrive at least an hour early. You'll need enough time to confirm arrangements with the treatment program and to take care of other contingencies. Make sure there will be no phone calls, knocks on the door, voices on the intercom, or other interruptions. Have participants take time to go over the agenda and compose themselves for the sequence of events.

Any refreshments must be finished, and containers discarded, before the leader shows participants to their seats.

Before the user arrives, remind everyone not to laugh, joke, chew gum, smoke, drink a beverage, drum their fingers, roll their eyes, exchange glances, or in any other way distract the user or each other from the topic at hand.

Your role as the professional facilitator

The designated leader cannot be expected to give the guidance and support that you, as a professional facilitator, can give. Without taking over, be prepared to apply your skills. *Your job is to make sure the concerned persons do what they have prepared themselves to do.*

The extreme anxiety provoked by the intervention process will require you to give a lot of reassurance, support, and encouragement—not only to the concerned persons, but also to the user. Because you're an advocate for everybody present, part of your responsibility is to foster an atmosphere of safety and respect that allows everyone to listen and be heard.

You cannot predict how participants will respond to the intervention, even after rehearsing it. Be prepared to help any or all of them deal with their feelings during and after the session. If you don't, the process will get hung up.

Emotions will run high. Participants' fears may intrude on your best-laid plans. Someone may start to weep. To help the group stay on track,

- **Make sure the user agrees not to respond until all the concerned persons have finished their statements.** If the leader forgets to secure this agreement, get it done before the intervenors start presenting their information. During the session the user will probably say something anyway. Be prepared with a reminder to wait until everyone has finished.

- **Don't rush things.** If a participant cries while talking, let the emotion take its course. Weeping can be powerful communication to the user.

- **When a participant feels threatened, offer support by identifying with the feeling:**

  > Lee, you seem frightened when you hear some of these concerns. I would too, if I were in your place. But remember we're here because we care about you.

- **Watch for enabling by the concerned persons.** As helpful as it is, rehearsing a presentation does not fully prepare one for the real thing. As the user begins showing signs of hurt, fear, or anger, concerned persons may start to change their intended presentations. Some may omit painful incidents or minimize their effect, letting the user off the hook. Some may say something to protect the user. Don't let these actions pass. Make the intervenor aware of what's happening:

  > Tony, I know you love Angela and don't want to see her hurt, and so you want us to understand why she turns to alcohol. But we're not here today to figure out why she drinks. We just want to let her know what her drinking is doing to her and to the people she cares about.

If the enabling contradicts something the speaker said earlier, point out the difference. Spontaneous changes in the planned presentations nearly always contain a contradiction. (This shows how important the written lists or letters are. They help keep the statements consistent when emotions run high.)

- Listen for "surrender words." They are subtle indicators of a willingness to accept treatment. If you miss them, the session will drag on past the point of effectiveness. Don't expect a user to say, "You're right! I see my drinking/using creates problems for us all, and so I want to go to treatment!" You have to pick up on cues that the user has, at least momentarily, opened the door:

    Boy, I don't know how I would tell my boss!

    How do you think the kids would do without me?

    I'll never be able to take the time off from work.

    When you hear a small hint that the user is open to accepting treatment, do not respond to the content of the statement. (Do not, for example, suggest how to inform the boss. Don't explain how the kids will be taken care of.) Simply reemphasize that treatment for chemical dependence is the most important thing in life right now.

What about ending the session without completing the presentations?

The goal of intervention is that the user will accept help. It's not that everyone will have a chance to talk. If surrender occurs before all presentations are finished, that is the time for immediate transition to the treatment program. Act while the window of opportunity is open, for it will close again quickly.

The remaining information (observations and feelings) should be presented and worked through later, during the evaluation and/or family counseling phase of the program.

Entering treatment

Whether surrender has come early or late in the session, the treatment program must be immediately informed that a structured intervention has taken place and then be given details. Efficient arrangements ahead of time, and efficient admission to the program, allow the treatment staff to take advantage of momentum. (See *The transition to treatment* earlier in this chapter.)

With the user, a counselor *must* process what happened during the intervention session and what the user's feelings are about it now. If this is done during or shortly after admission—while the information is fresh— the counselor can reinforce the feelings of surrender and can help the expression of anger or feelings of betrayal, while keeping the person mindful of the damage the alcohol/drug use is doing. Having this information freshly in mind can save days or weeks of effort to retrieve it in the treatment process. A similar post-intervention session should also be conducted with the spouse/partner/close friend. (See *Helping the concerned persons process the content of the session and make decisions about their future,* below.)

NOTE: After treatment is completed, the counselor should revisit the intervention session with the user, to reinforce how necessary the treatment was for all concerned.

If the treatment facility offers a family counseling program and a group for other intervenors, those who care about the chemically dependent person will also benefit from the treatment process in a more complete way. If there are no such ancillary programs, or if some of the intervenors don't join them, the counselor must get a signed release from the user—who is now a client of the facility—allowing the counselor to get confidential information from those who participated in the intervention.

F. Helping the concerned persons process the content of the session and make decisions about their future

A post-intervention session with the concerned persons is important because no matter what happens in the session, they'll need to be reminded that *intervention is a process, not an event*. If the user agrees to enter treatment, the process doesn't stop there. For their own sake and for the user's sake, the concerned persons must continue listing observations and feelings. They must also stop enabling the use of alcohol/drugs and work at not getting enmeshed again in denial and dysfunctional behavior.

If the user leaves immediately for treatment, have the remaining family members take time to describe their feelings, summarize what they've learned, and look ahead to what they will do as treatment progresses. If working through the experience and looking ahead will take longer (which they probably will), make arrangements for another meeting. Participants need a sense of closure on the first phase and a chance to anticipate the next one.

Be sure to get in touch with the family members who accompanied the user to treatment, so that they too can process their feelings, review what they have learned, and look ahead. Plan for one or more appointments in your office.

If the user refuses to accept treatment

If the user does not accept treatment or any of the other stipulations set forth by the group, end the session with a positive statement anyway. Mention that everyone has gathered out of love and concern, and that they will continue to feel that love and concern. Have the escort accompany the user back to their meeting place.

With the remaining participants, bring closure by reviewing what *has* been gained. Remind participants of all they have learned about the disease of chemical dependence. The family, especially, needs your professional assurance that they are not responsible for the illness—and that they must make their own decisions: decisions that do not depend on the actions or approval of the user. They must go on with their own lives and follow through on the action plans to which they have committed themselves. (See step 4 of *The six steps of an effective intervention* in Chapter 1.)

Also remind participants of the role assigned to those who, for whatever reason, did not participate in person. They also did their part. They are not to be blamed for the user's refusing to accept help.

Be sure that those who did not participate in person are informed of the outcome and are told that the user's refusal to accept help is not their fault.

All participants need to understand that this is not necessarily the last intervention. Although the prospect may seem bleak, the awareness heightened by shared experiences may lay the foundation for another attempt. If the concerned persons are so disappointed that they "don't care one way or the other anymore," end on a positive note without dismissing their feelings. The disappointment can be addressed later in your office.

Remember that the concerned persons who got in touch with you are still your clients. They will require your continued support.

If at first you don't succeed ...

Keep trying! A well-planned intervention is successful even if the user does not accept the recommended treatment. Participants have gained insights they can use to help themselves and others. And proper preparation lays the groundwork for future interventions.

Remember: *Intervention is a process, not a single event.* The structured intervention session is by no means the end of it. If the user is not moved to accept treatment right away, the effect can nevertheless be profound. In time, the information and concern expressed in that meeting will sink in; or crises will build until the user decides that something must be done. If the concerned persons gather again to present their observations and express their feelings, they will probably succeed in getting the user into treatment. But even if they don't, their new understanding of the disease will help stop their habits of enabling and will encourage them to lead healthy lives.

Whether or not the user ever accepts treatment, the professional must continue to help family members dismantle the *enabling family system* and support the members as they make their own decisions about their health and recovery.

CHAPTER 3

A Model for Formal Intervention Programming

Introduction

Intervention as described in this book can be facilitated by any helping-professional who is well-informed about chemical dependence, its effects on the family, and the intervention process. So far, we've discussed working with one group at a time.

If you offer services to a large number of clients whose problems stem from the use of alcohol or other drugs, consider creating a *formal intervention program* that will allow you to help more people in the same amount of time. The education you now provide to single groups of concerned persons will be conducted in classes containing several different groups. (The pre-intervention, intervention, and post-intervention sessions will remain private.)

Why place clients together in classes and groups?

There are distinct advantages in having groups of concerned persons—especially several families—learning about chemical dependence together:[1]

- In a group, clients see there are other people like them, with similar problems, similar emotions, similar hopes. They see they are not alone. This recognition reduces feelings of embarrassment, isolation, loneliness, and fear.

- Group sessions help to eliminate stereotypes of chemically dependent people. Clients come to realize that many other regular citizens are chemically dependent—including many they admire.

- Group synergy motivates all members. Participants encourage and support each another.

- Group members learn a vocabulary that helps them tackle the problem. When, for example, participants notice that a spouse employs *denial* as a defense, just as the user does, there's a word for it. When a sibling *enables* by making excuses for the user, there's a word for it. When a grandparent refers to the *disease* of chemical dependence, there's no longer disbelief that such a condition exists. Through an enriched vocabulary, understanding grows.

---

[1] It's appropriate to include close friends—and essential if a user has no family.

A formal intervention program

In designing a program for groups, consider these key components of the Intervention Program Model developed by the Johnson Institute:[2]

Client flow

Remember that the client is rarely the user. Almost always the primary client is the concerned person who seeks help; the one who gets in touch with you. As a group, the other concerned persons are also your clients.

In a formal intervention program, the primary client would generally receive the following sequence of service. Ordinarily the other concerned persons would be brought into the process at step 5, after the primary client's private session with an intervention counselor.

1. **Initial contact.** The client nearly always telephones the agency. Very few clients are walk-ins. Whoever is on the switchboard must be well prepared to handle the call. A concerned person is generally suffering from fear, confusion, and other painful emotions, as well as from a burden of misinformation. The call must be answered by someone who is competent and understanding and who *sounds* competent and understanding. This person must be able to tactfully stop the caller from blurting out the whole story. This person must also be ready to answer the caller's questions, support the decision to get help, and make a referral to the appropriate resource— usually to the intake counselor.

---

[2] For more information about the Intervention Program Model, call Johnson Institute toll-free: 1-800-231-5165.

2. **Intake counseling.** The intake counselor listens to the client's story, then explains the services in general (to the primary client alone or to the primary client and other concerned persons). If the agency/client match seems suitable, the intake counselor makes two appointments for the client: 1) to attend an education session, and 2) to meet privately with an intervention counselor. It's best if everyone at the education session can talk with a counselor immediately afterward.

3. **Education session.** One-hour meetings are scheduled at set times for groups of new clients to learn more about chemical dependence and what can be done about it. This gives them a chance to know what they're dealing with before deciding to continue. (See *The education session* later in this chapter.)

4. **Private session with an intervention counselor.** With information from the intake counselor, and in consultation with the client(s), the intervention counselor assesses the need for intervention and each client's readiness to participate. Clients who are ready are assigned to a family intervention class. Those who are not ready are referred to a concerned persons group. (See *The private session with an intervention counselor* later in this chapter.)

5. **Family intervention class *or* concerned persons group.** Family members, close friends, and other meaningful concerned persons who appear ready to begin planning an intervention are assigned to a class for instruction, for preparation of lists or letters to be read to the user, and for decisions contingent on the user's acceptance or refusal

of treatment. This intervention class may be intertwined with the rehearsal. (See *The family intervention class* and *The pre-intervention session*, later in this chapter.)

Some clients (whether spouses or teenage or adult children) may not be ready to participate effectively without special help. The intervention counselor and the other concerned persons must decide whether to conduct the intervention session without them. Clients immobilized by fear, shame, denial—and sometimes delusion— are often so enmeshed with the user that they've lost all perspective. They'll not be ready to practice, or even accept, the basic tenets of intervention until they have received the education and support of a concerned persons group. (See *The concerned persons group* later in this chapter.)

Those who are excluded from the structured intervention *must* be included in other meaningful ways throughout the process. To leave them out can invite sabotage and scapegoating. If the user does not enter treatment, the excluded people may be blamed.

6. **Pre-intervention session.** This is the practice session. It's a chance to role-play the event and discover what needs to be remedied before the actual structured intervention. It usually takes two or three hours. It may be intertwined with the family intervention class. (See *The pre-intervention session* later in this chapter.)

7. **Structured intervention session.** Family members and other concerned persons confront

the user with statements of their observations and feelings, then present their recommendations for treatment. The user responds and either accepts help or rejects it.

8. **Post-intervention session.** This is a private meeting between the facilitator and the family and other concerned persons when the structured intervention session is over. (See *The post-intervention session* later in this chapter.)

The education session

This general meeting can be scheduled as frequently as necessary to accommodate the number of groups you have. Its content is simple and straightforward. Plan to cover it in a couple of hours, depending on the size of the group and the number of questions you expect to answer. Without going into detail, discuss—

- The disease concept of chemical dependence

- Genetic influences

- The *Feeling Chart* of Dr. Vernon E. Johnson,[3] tracing the progress of the disease

- How the disease affects people living or working with the user

- Enabling: what it is and how concerned persons get caught up in it

- Treatment: why it is effective and desirable; how to get it

---

[3] See Appendix A.

- General information about intervention; policy stating the role of the professional

Even to some clients who are ready to proceed, the details of intervention can be too threatening. Cover the details later, in the family intervention class.

Do acknowledge the courage the participants have demonstrated by seeking help. Assure them that it's normal to feel ambivalent, angry, fearful, embarrassed, and guilty about the problems they're facing. Tell them they can credit themselves for having the concern and courage to listen and learn—while millions of other people like them around the world will continue suffering needlessly because they won't take action.

At the end of the session, ask the clients whether they already have an appointment with an intervention counselor. (The intake counselor should already have taken care of this. See step 2 of *Client flow*, above.) Anyone without an appointment needs to make one now.

The private session with an intervention counselor

Have this appointment made during intake, so that each client at the education session can talk with a counselor immediately afterward, while thoughts are fresh. During this one-to-one meeting, the intervention counselor will

- Review the ideas presented in the education session and assess how well the client heard and accepted them

- Help the client verbalize specific concerns about things going on in the client's life

- Help the client identify his or her own role in the situations that are causing concern

- Determine whether the family and the user exhibit behavior associated with the disease of chemical dependence

- Decide whether intervention would be appropriate, and how soon. Is the client able? Is the client willing? Does the client have a sufficient number of concerned persons ready and able to join in confronting the user? Which persons who are meaningful to the user can be encouraged to attend family intervention classes, or at least come in and talk with an intervention counselor (even though they may not be family members)?

- Help the ready and able client develop a plan of action. Out-of-towners who cannot attend this session can be referred to a similar one where they live. They can later join the group for the rehearsal and the intervention session.

- For the client who seems unable to accept—or even hear—the information about the disease process; for the client who is unwilling to try to get other concerned persons involved in intervention; and for the client who appears emotionally immobilized or unstable, suggest referral to the concerned persons group, to Al-Anon, or to another appropriate resource, such as a psychiatrist, psychologist, or clinical social worker.

The family intervention class

This class is for groups of family members,[4] close friends, and other meaningful concerned persons who are emotionally able and ready to participate in a structured intervention. The class provides

- Information about the disease of chemical dependence

- Instruction on the principles and process of intervention

- Support from family members and close friends of other users, assuring everyone in the class that they are not alone

- Guidance in forming an intervention team

- Assistance in preparing for a structured intervention

The family intervention class is ideally three sessions in a single week, but usually it's less than that. The ideal can serve as a guide:

Session 1. In the first meeting, clients learn about the *disease process* of chemical dependence and how it affects not only the user, but also the concerned persons and others whose lives are touched by the user. Clients also learn to recognize *enabling*. (Some of this will already be familiar to those who attended the education session shortly after intake.)

At this stage of the formal intervention program, instruction is geared toward action. Clients are helped to

---

[4] Family members should usually be at least ten years old, depending on maturity.

apply their new knowledge as they plan their structured interventions. Content includes—

- The signs, symptoms, and progression of the disease of chemical dependence. The *Feeling Chart.*

- Denial and delusion. Value conflicts. Enabling. Family dysfunction.

- Large-group discussion in which participants describe how they feel—and hear how others feel—so as to break through denial and feelings of being different from other families, and to lessen the sense of isolation those feelings create.

- Small-group discussion of questions such as, *What evidence of denial and delusion have you seen in the chemically dependent person? How have these defenses affected you and your family? What are some of the ways you have enabled the person to continue drinking or using?*

- Information on the kinds of treatment available in the area. Examples of people who have received help through treatment and A.A. and other Twelve-Step recovery groups, and how their lives have changed; how the lives of family members, friends, employers, and coworkers have been affected by these changes.

- The principles of intervention. This presentation is more detailed than the one in the earlier education session. Participants start writing their lists (and letters) and start planning just how they will do the intervening.

Session 2. This meeting is almost entirely audiovisual. Participants can view videos such as *Back to Reality;*

Enabling: Masking Reality; and *Intervention: Facing Reality*. These videos show how chemical dependence progresses and how concerned persons can address it by effectively planning the use of certain techniques. Participants are asked to watch for examples of enabling and to notice how the techniques of intervention are employed. Discussion helps clarify and reinforce the messages.

Session 3. Concerned persons gather in groups to role-play a successful structured intervention with simulated information. (Those who are concerned about a particular user need not all join the same group. The important thing is that everyone has a chance to observe and participate in role-playing before the real rehearsal and the actual intervention session.)

The facilitator instructs the leader and other group members before starting to monitor the action.

After the role-playing, the facilitator gives feedback, as will be done after role-playing at the real rehearsal with each private group. For example,

- Did the leader arrange for proper seating?

- Did the leader ask the chemically dependent person not to respond until members had presented their information?

- Did the concerned persons present both observations and feelings?

- Did they avoid gossip and second-hand information?

- Did they use precise words to make clear what they meant?

- Did they sound caring and concerned, rather than angry?

- Did they avoid enabling the user by excusing, minimizing, rationalizing, and so forth?

- Did the leader present the group's recommendation for treatment?

- Was the treatment program prepared to accept the referral immediately?

To improve their own presentations, participants should be invited to give each other feedback too. Their comments can be integrated with the facilitator's or saved until later. In either case, the facilitator must listen carefully to make sure their understanding is correct.

Before the last session adjourns, make sure each group has an appointment for a private post-intervention session with the facilitator immediately following their private structured intervention.

The concerned persons group

This group is for clients who appear too immobilized or unstable to contribute to—or benefit from—a structured intervention.[5] They're usually drawn from several different groups of clients preparing to intervene with different users. What they all have in common is that they are so enmeshed in their problem that they cannot accept, or even hear, the facts of the matter. Their own denial, other emotional problems, or strong feelings render them incapable of proceeding with an intervention

---

[5] Members of the group should be at least ten years old, depending on maturity.

at this time. Some may exhibit full-blown codependence (see below). In any case, they won't be ready until they have dealt with their own problems.

It may or may not be wise to delay intervention until a concerned person is ready. That decision is up to those who are willing and able to proceed, in consultation with the intervention counselor and, preferably, with the person in question.

Whenever a concerned person is omitted from the group, that person *and* the intervenors must understand the reason. As mentioned earlier, the absent person must also be able to participate in a meaningful way. To shut anyone out is to invite sabotage and scapegoating.

Characteristics of a codependent

For more information about clients who are not appropriate to include in intervention because their dysfunction is typical of full-blown codependence, read *Diagnosing and Treating Codependence*, by Timmen L. Cermak, M.D., published by the Johnson Institute.[6] Says Dr. Cermak, "Power through sacrifice of self lies at the core of codependence."

Dr. Cermak explains how a helping-professional can recognize full-blown codependence. See Part Two of his book for discussion of these criteria:

A. Continued investment of self-esteem in the ability to control oneself and others in the face of serious adverse consequences.

This involves a distorted relationship to willpower; a confusion of identities; denial; and low self-esteem.

---

[6] See Appendix C, *Johnson Institute Resources for Programming.* For more information, call Johnson Institute toll-free: 1-800-231-5165.

Distorted relationship to willpower. Codependents tend to believe they can overcome their own feelings and behavior—as well as the feelings and behavior of the chemically dependent person—by sheer force of will. ("If only we all try hard enough and pull together, we can get your father to stop drinking.") Failure to achieve such control leads to a sense of inadequacy. Ashamed to ask for help, codependents become more and more isolated and dysfunctional.

Confusion of identities. The sense of self is compromised and even lost. Says Dr. Cermak, "The codependent's self-worth rises or falls with his or her partner's success or failure." Enmeshed in a relationship with a chemically dependent person, the codependent feels responsible for making the user happy and for making the user stay sober. The codependent who is not in a relationship feels an internal void.

Denial. The codependent person either consciously or unconsciously chooses not to see the user's inappropriate behavior—or finds reasons for personal failure to keep the user from using. ("I didn't try hard enough ... I didn't try long enough ... I tried the wrong way.") Says Dr. Cermak, "The denial of the chemical dependent and the denial of the codependent are the same. Both work to preserve the status quo."

Low self-esteem. A codependent tends to give other people power over his or her own self-esteem. Unable to keep the user happy and sober, and unable to see the futility and harm of trying to do so, the codependent determines to try even harder. Repeated failures heighten the person's sense of inadequacy.

Both a cause and an effect of codependence, low self-esteem tends to lead the codependent person into self-destructive relationships and to keep the person stuck there, no matter how painful.

B. Assumption of responsibility for meeting others' needs to the exclusion of acknowledging one's own.

Codependents carry generosity to the extreme: self-sacrifice. To avoid making the chemically dependent person unhappy, the codependent denies his or her own needs, preferences, and feelings. ("What would you like to do this weekend?" "Whatever *you'd* like to do.") A codependent wife and mother who won't let her children scream at each other will allow her husband and children to scream at her. At the root of such behavior is the fear of being abandoned. According to Dr. Cermak, "Codependents tend to choose one extreme or another: denial of themselves to keep someone else happy, or compulsive avoidance of others to keep themselves safe."

C. Anxiety and boundary distortions around intimacy and separation.

According to Dr. Cermak, "The codependent equates closeness with compliance and intimacy with fusion. As he or she becomes more involved with another person, the tendency is to take on many of that person's values, wishes, dreams, and characteristics, and eventually much of his or her denial system. The codependent becomes a mirror. ... The codependent involved with a chemical dependent actually feels that person's pain, rather than feeling empathy for the pain. This helps to fill the void which results from not honoring one's own needs and feelings."

D. Enmeshment in relationships with personality disordered, chemically dependent, other codependent, and/or impulse disordered individuals.

The defense mechanisms of rationalization, projection, and denial are typical of adolescents—and typical of adult codependents and chemically dependent people who are not in recovery. Says Dr. Cermak, "When the codependent is confronted with immature defenses in others, he or she responds by mirroring them." There's a mutual attraction that those involved call "chemistry" or "falling in love."

When the relationship breaks up, the codependent copes with the blow to self-esteem by resolving to try harder to make the next relationship work.

E. Three or more of these ten characteristics:

1. Excessive reliance on denial. Both chemical dependence and codependence are diseases of denial—tuning out certain internal and external realities. Denial is largely an unconscious process, employed to achieve a sense of security.

Any chemically dependent person can point to symptoms that she or he does not display. And because symptoms of codependence are also many, no one individual will display them all. The "missing" symptoms may be cited as evidence that no problem exists. The amount of delusion and denial maintained by a codependent can equal or exceed that of the chemically dependent person.

According to Dr. Cermak, "Codependents frequently see the breakdown of their denial system as a sign of their own personal inadequacy, much as chemical dependents view their growing lack of control over alcohol/drugs as a sign of personal weakness."

2. Constriction of emotions. To prove they can maintain at least a semblance of control over their lives, many families in the early stages of treatment believe they must curb their emotions. "Typically," says Dr. Cermak, "the emotions they work hardest to restrict are those normally considered to be immature, dangerous, uncomfortable, or just plain bad: anger, fear, sadness, rage, embarrassment, bitterness, loneliness, etc. Unfortunately, it is impossible to put a lid on such 'negative' feelings without also impeding the expression of more positive ones, such as happiness."

This is one reason that the second half of Al-Anon's First Step is so important to codependents: "We admitted… that our lives had become unmanageable." Codependents are deeply dedicated to "managing" their lives and the lives of others.

Outbursts of pent-up rage and verbalizing every feeling as it comes may appear to contradict the symptomatic constriction of feelings—but their purpose is the same, says Dr. Cermak: to lessen the anxiety of dealing with feelings.

3. Depression. "Anger turned inward, unresolved grief, the chronic restraint of feelings, being identified more with one's false self than one's true self—codependents have plenty of reasons to be depressed," according to Dr. Cermak. "Typically, however, they view their depression as evidence of inadequacy and the failure to stay in control, and for this reason they usually deny its presence."

Also, "admitting that one is depressed means admitting that one has needs, and codependents, by definition, always place the needs of others above their own in importance."

4. Hypervigilance. "The codependent's environment is unpredictable, basically incomprehensible, and highly stressful. ... The only way for the codependent to survive is by being ultrasensitive to subtle shifts in a chemical dependent's behavior and mood," Dr. Cermak says. "Such hypervigilance is a recognized symptom of Post Traumatic Stress Disorder (PTSD), which is most typically seen in combat veterans."

This is related to the codependent's need to control how other people feel and behave—and the need to attend to other people's happiness in order to feel good about oneself.

5. Compulsions. Codependents tend to involve themselves in a great deal of compulsive behavior. They might overeat, overwork, gamble, read voraciously, seek sex, rescue others, be intensely involved in religion, or use alcohol/drugs (see #7, below). Some watch television constantly and worry if they miss an episode of their favorite program; others clean the house incessantly— all in an effort to forestall uncomfortable, threatening feelings.

Just as a chemically dependent person must abstain from alcohol/drugs in order to recover, a codependent must abstain from the compulsion.

6. Anxiety. "The anxiety of codependence can take a variety of forms, from free-floating, chronic anxiety to panic attacks, phobias, and existential dread," says Dr. Cermak. The anxiety stems largely from the high level of denial the codependent must maintain.

7. Abuse of alcohol or other drugs. Many codependents develop a compulsive use of alcohol, diet pills, tranquilizers, and other mind-altering substances with addictive potential. Dr. Cermak points out that "denial is necessary to avoid being overwhelmed by feelings, and substance abuse serves as a biochemical 'booster' for one's crumbling denial."

Chemical dependence and codependence are not two distinct problems. "The denial of the chemical dependent and the denial of the codependent are cut from the same cloth." When a codependent is treated for chemical dependence, "the underlying codependence must not be ignored."

8. History of physical and/or sexual abuse. Many codependents have been or are now the victims of actual or threatened physical and/or sexual abuse. Sometimes the abuse takes place during a blackout—which means the abuser has no memory of it and, consequently, no feelings of guilt.

Dr. Cermak notes, "Codependents tend to minimize both the amount of violence in their relationships and the level of stress they live under. They do not see themselves as victims of physical or sexual abuse except in the most extreme cases, and even then they frequently take the blame: either they 'caused' the abuse or they 'deserve' to be treated abusively. Especially if few or no overtly abusive acts have occurred, the codependent's denial system prevents him or her from viewing the situation realistically." ("My husband is good to me. Whenever he hits me, he only uses his hand. He never uses a board or anything that could do any real damage.")

Children who are physically and/or sexually abused are often unaware that it's wrong and that it is not their fault. The feelings stirred by the abuse continue into adulthood.

"One of the most reliable symptoms of codependence," says Dr. Cermak, "is the inability to leave a chronically abusive relationship behind, whether that relationship is ongoing or past."

It may be dangerous, if not life-threatening, for a codependent to attempt intervention with a user who is physically abusive. (See *When is intervention not appropriate?* in Chapter 4.)

9. Stress-related medical illnesses. Like other people who have dysfunctional reactions to stress, codependents have more tension headaches, migraine headaches, asthma, hypertension, strokes, gastritis, peptic ulcers, spastic colon, rheumatoid arthritis, and sexual dysfunction than the general population. Some codependents are so adept at denying the stress of their home lives that physical illness may take decades to appear.

10. Staying in a relationship with an active substance abuser for at least two years without seeking outside help. Dr. Cermak proposes a limit of two years to make sure that failure to seek help signifies active codependence, rather than a normal desire to handle personal problems in one's own way.

Attitude and content of the concerned persons group

The concerned persons group may be structured as a limited number of sessions or left open-ended. It can help its members by

- Creating a supportive atmosphere in which participants are encouraged to gain strength and understanding

- Creating an opportunity for participants to gain insights that increase self-confidence and self-respect

- Providing education about chemical dependence and codependence

- Teaching principles of intervention, and encouraging participants to proceed with an intervention when they are ready and able to do so

In Part Three of *Diagnosing and Treating Codependence*, Dr. Cermak offers many suggestions for working with codependents. Those with full-blown codependence may need months of group counseling and individual counseling to become ready to take even minor steps toward eliminating their enabling actions and participating in a structured intervention. It should be remembered, however, that many codependents *can* be very effective participants.

The knowledge that change can take a long time may be a danger in itself, for both the chemically dependent person and the codependent. The helping-professional must take care not to enable codependents to stay in unhealthy relationships by expanding the number of counseling sessions. They must stay focused on the primary goal of intervention: helping the user to accept treatment before it's too late.

The pre-intervention session

In this private session, clients concerned about a user make final preparations for their structured intervention. (For details see *Guiding the concerned persons through an intervention role-playing* and *Facilitating the intervention session*, in Chapter 2.)

You can expect some of the participants to regress during rehearsal. They may feel paralyzed by fear. They may start to doubt that intervention is possible. Old attitudes may emerge. ("It's a moral problem." "It's really my fault." "It's just that she has so many pressures in her life.") If this happens, you must take time for reeducation. Remind the clients of other things group members have said and they've agreed with. Mention facts and feelings they themselves have described. Let them know it's normal to feel like backing off; it would be a rare group that didn't feel doubt and fear at this point. Reiterate how important it is to get help for the user. Be sure to reinforce expressions of hope for changes in their lives.

Let all group members know they're not expected to do a perfect job of intervening. Assure them that you and the other participants will be there to support anyone who feels hesitant or shaky.

The post-intervention session

Whether or not the user accepts treatment, this important meeting takes place with the family and other concerned persons immediately after the intervention. If some of them accompany the user to a treatment program, use your judgment about delaying the session. It should be held the same day.

With emphasis on the needs of family members, the purposes of the session are

- To help participants process their thoughts and feelings about the intervention

- To help them assess the information presented, identify what was omitted, and decide what still needs to be said and when

- To help them stand by their commitments to their own recovery regardless of the user's response to intervention; to help them identify the difficulties they may encounter and how they will handle them

- To help them analyze what happened as a result of their group effort; to discuss whether to try intervention again

- To *celebrate* what the family members, the other concerned persons, and the facilitator have accomplished, such as
  1) helping the user accept treatment or at least begin to see the need for treatment, 2) raising awareness of their power to make effective choices for themselves, whether or not the user accepts treatment, and 3) learning constructive behavior that will aid their own progress in recovery

Now is the time to remind those who care for the user that *intervention is a process, not a single event.* It's time to mobilize for the future by highlighting the changes that have already taken place and the changes that need to take place as the process continues.

Contrasting conditions *before* and *after*

To show the family members what they have accomplished, use a marker board or flip chart so members actually see where they were before, where they are now, and where they are headed because they cared enough to intervene. Here are some changes family members often cite:

Before: They thought they had few rights as individuals and as members of the family.

Now: They know they have rights and can exercise them without feeling guilty or disloyal.

Before: Their personal boundaries were blurred, or even nonexistent.

Now: They know who they are and how to set boundaries within and outside the family.

Before: They judged themselves by external standards (other people's values).

Now: They validate themselves according to their own, internal values and standards.

Before: They perceived that only certain members of the family were important and valued within the family.

Now: The perception is that all family members are equally important and valued.

Before: They often hid the truth.

Now: They can speak out honestly and value themselves for it.

Before: Family members felt hopeless.

Now: They feel hopeful.

The contrast between *before* and *after* helps family members feel good about themselves—and appreciate each other—for acknowledging their pain and dealing with it honestly. The family has acted effectively as a unit to solve a difficult problem, and it can do it again and again, because its members have learned to tap their own power and resources.

Bringing a sense of closure

After the intervention, participants need a sense of closure. This does not mean bringing the process to an end. Personal issues raised during the process will not have had time to be resolved.

Urge participants to continue in a recovery program to address these issues, as well as family matters, in order to live comfortably in a healthy family system. Make referrals and provide assistance for a smooth transition to a family counseling program or to psychotherapy, individual counseling, Al-Anon, Adult Children of Alcoholics, or another appropriate service.

An important topic for the post-intervention session is separation. Participants need to be prepared for temporary separation from their chemically dependent loved one—and for separation from the counselor on whom they've come to depend. The counselor needs to explain how his or her relationship will continue with the concerned persons and with the user.

In reaching closure, families will at times credit the counselor for the good things that have come from the intervention process. *This is an opportunity for the counselor to give that credit back to the family; to validate their decision to use their rightful power to begin restoring themselves to health.*

Adapting the Intervention Program Model

The formal intervention program has been used and refined by the Johnson Institute for more than three decades. It has been used successfully by helping-professionals in thousands of widely diverse counseling agencies, clinics, treatment centers, and other organizations, and in private practice.

The program can be modified to suit many different circumstances. Cultural, economic, and logistic requirements can all be accommodated.

Individuals and organizations interested in training by the Johnson Institute are invited to call the Institute toll-free.[7]

---

[7] The Johnson Institute provides Intervention Training Seminars for helping-professionals. The seminars include practical help in adapting the intervention program for any setting. Call 1-800-231-5165.

CHAPTER 4

Questions About Intervention

For more than three decades, structured intervention has been used by helping-professionals in many different settings, with many different kinds of clients. It is not a static or rigid process. It is continually being refined to accommodate the realities of modern life. Questions like these from helping-professionals lead to the ever-growing effectiveness of the process and techniques:

How do I select a qualified facilitator?

The Johnson Institute has prepared a list of *Standards for the Professional Interventionist*. See Appendix B.

How does intervention work with different populations?

The process and techniques of intervention were first developed with middle-class, middle-aged, married, white male alcoholics. But thousands of women, single people, gays and lesbians, persons of color, young people, and others dependent on the use of alcohol/drugs and other addictive behavior have since benefited from the process described in this book. Addicted people are more alike than different, and so are those who care about them.

Nevertheless, an intervention program should be designed to fit the needs and characteristics of the concerned persons and the users. Interventionists must be ready to modify their approaches with previously underserved (and overlapping) populations, such as professionals, single parents, immigrants, victims of abuse, people with physical disabilities, members of ethnic minority groups, people living alone, people without families, senior adults, and—when appropriate—children.

Status is sometimes an issue in assigning people to groups. People with power and authority don't always relate well to people they don't consider their peers. Physicians, some other professionals, and top-level business executives tend to listen only to others like themselves. Typically it doesn't work to mix physicians with nonphysicians, or CEOs with workers of lesser rank. But today there are many professional groups with names such as Accountants Concerned for Accountants, Lawyers Concerned for Lawyers, and Physicians Concerned for Physicians, to assist with professional peer teams. They can be located through the professional's local, state, and national associations.

Over the past three decades, helping-professionals who are also recovering alcoholics/addicts have added many effective techniques to the original process of intervention.

In a similar way, professionals who are part of a minority group can be very effective in adapting the process to the cultural realities of the group.

When is intervention *not* appropriate?

Structured intervention is not appropriate for every case of chemical dependence. When, for example, an alcoholic husband is a wife beater, it may be dangerous, if not life-threatening, for her to attempt an intervention. A counselor should *not* lead a victim of physical/sexual abuse to think the problem can be solved by intervening and getting the user into treatment. It's not that simple. Although an abuser may be more likely to strike out when drunk or high, it cannot be said that the alcohol/drug use is causing the violent behavior. The concerned person should be referred to a counseling agency for victims of abuse, as well as to Al-Anon.

When spouses are involved in a bitter divorce or custody battle, it is not appropriate for one spouse to initiate an intervention on the other. Motives may be suspect. Anyway, the low level of trust between them would interfere with the caring, concerned, nonaccusatory communication required for a successful intervention.

Most important, if the user or any concerned person seems suicidal, intervention must be postponed until the safety of everyone can be reasonably assured.

Can intervention be used with adolescents?

This intervention model has been used with adolescents, but experience has shown the process is more complicated than it is with adults. Without a long history of chemical use, or without evidence that the adolescent has been unable to stop using, a structured intervention may be premature.

For adolescents, the process of intervention (that is, intervening without a regular structured intervention) needs to begin *earlier* than it ordinarily does, because chemical use in itself has serious legal implications for people that age. If a young person is caught using drugs on or near the school grounds, for instance, the immediate response should be the school's disciplinary policy, coupled with education about the effects of chemical abuse, rather than a major intervention followed by treatment.

For a comprehensive description of how parents and professionals can use intervention effectively with adolescents, read *Choices and Consequences: How to Use Intervention with Teenagers in Trouble with Alcohol/Drugs, a Step-By-Step Guide for Parents and Professionals*, by Dick Schaefer, published by the Johnson Institute.[1]

Is surprise really important? Is it ethical?

Sometimes the intervention process is criticized as sneaky or demeaning because it appears to go behind the back of the chemically dependent person.

Intervention need not be a complete surprise. In many cases the user knows for weeks that a loved one is going for counseling and that it has to do with concerns about the use of alcohol or other drugs. Often the using has led to serious arguments and scenes in which members of the household have begged the user to stop.

Note that in the treatment of mental illness, *transparency* (a patient's awareness of the strategy and techniques that will be used to aid recovery) is not necessarily a hindrance to treatment. In treating chemical dependence, it's probably not as important as many professionals think it is to keep the planned intervention a secret. Often the user, perhaps anticipating

---

[1] This book is a companion piece for the video *Choices and Consequences: Intervention with Youth in Trouble with Alcohol/Drugs*, also produced by the Johnson Institute. The video dramatically portrays how parents and professionals working together can use intervention to deal successfully with all levels of chemical use by young people. (See Appendix C, *Johnson Institute Resources for Programming*.) For more information call the Institute toll-free: 1-800-231-5165.

some sort of confrontation, attempts to curb the alcohol/drug use before being approached.

In planning an intervention it's important that you, the professional, not allow yourself to be pressured into using any technique that is incompatible with your own philosophy, methods, or personal value system. If you think the chemically dependent person should be told that the drinking/drug use has become the focus of your counseling with the client, you must tell the client so and reach a decision. If you think the user should know who will attend the intervention session, stand by your beliefs. Over time you will find that your own approach works just fine in certain kinds of situations. Avoid those that will conflict with your sense of what is appropriate and effective. Keep your actions congruent with your professional values. As a role model, you owe it to your clients.

What if I can't get the concerned persons together soon?

Sometimes geographic distance, military duty, or other circumstances make it difficult to get the most meaningful concerned persons together for the planning and for the meeting with the user. When intervenors are available for only a brief visit, you may have to pare the process down to its bare essentials.

Many hastily prepared interventions are not successful. They should be tried only if the seriousness of the user's condition warrants it and if other options have been exhausted.

To make the best of the situation: Arrange for those with schedule conflicts to attend a family intervention class and work with an interventionist in their own area until it's time for the rehearsal and the intervention session.[2] If necessary, they can send a videotape/audiotape or letter to the user, to be presented at the intervention.

Or they might be sent some educational material, such as the Johnson Institute's *Family Intervention Primer*,[3] and be helped to prepare by phone. When they arrive, the information session might be pared to a one-hour talk on the *Feeling Chart* and the nature of denial and delusion. The concerned persons' lists of information (observations and feelings) would be written quickly, and the role playing/rehearsal would be brief.

This paring-down and speeding-up can work if there are no serious impediments such as a dysfunctional spouse, a friend who decides at the last minute to support the user against the spouse, or fear on the part of concerned persons about taking action so fast.

Most important, use your experience and good judgment to decide whether hurrying the intervention will achieve the primary purpose of any intervention: to get the user the needed help before it's too late.

My clients who are members of Al-Anon will say they have no need to intervene because they have detached themselves from the problem.

Al-Anon is extremely worthwhile. It helps those living with a chemically dependent person understand and accept that they are not the cause of the alcohol/drug use; that they are not responsible for any of that behavior; and that they must carry on with their lives regardless of what the chemically dependent person does.

---

[2] National Council on Alcoholism and Drug Dependence (NCADD) offices throughout the United States can assist. Write to 12 West 21st Street, New York, NY 10010. Or phone (212) 206-6770.

[3] This kit is listed in Appendix C, *Johnson Institute Resources for Programming*. For further information call the Institute toll-free: 1-800-231-5165.

Some Al-Anon members, however, misinterpret the message as meaning that chemically dependent persons are sick from a disease and therefore cannot be held responsible for their actions. In seeking to become detached from the user's problems, these Al-Anon members become passive. They don't understand that the second part of the Serenity Prayer (*the courage to change the things I can*) implies that sometimes one must take direct action with the user.

To deal effectively with clients who have taken the passive way out, you must be familiar with the Al-Anon literature. In it are many statements urging people to change what can be changed *before* they accept the things that cannot be changed.[4] Compassion dictates that you respectfully confront clients about their misinterpretations of the Al-Anon message. You might, for instance, draw an analogy: If a diabetic refuses to take the required insulin and falls into a coma, the responsibility for the problem is solely the diabetic's.

A client who is extremely codependent will probably continue to distort the Al-Anon message even after the concepts have been clarified again and again. This client needs to be gently confronted each time this thinking is expressed—and be shown a realistic, healthier way of looking at the situation. The booklet *Detachment vs. Intervention: Is There a Conflict?* (published by the Johnson Institute and approved by the Al-Anon Family Group Headquarters) is an excellent tool for helping concerned persons understand that detachment and intervention are not mutually exclusive ideas; that they are, in fact, a powerful agent for change when properly integrated.[5]

---

[4] The order of mention in the *Serenity Prayer* notwithstanding. (See *Afterword.*)

[5] See Appendix C, *Johnson Institute Resources for Programming*. For more information call the Institute toll-free: 1-800-231-5165.

Who pays for intervention? Will insurance companies pay for it if they pay for treatment?

Insurance companies seldom pay for interventions that take place before formal admission into a treatment program. The day has not yet come when intervention is seen as an essential contribution to the health-care delivery system, reimbursable in its own right.

If the insurance company refuses to cover an intervention, you might suggest that the client get in touch with the state insurance commissioner about it.

What's the point of doing an intervention after a person has entered treatment?

At any stage of the recovery process, a person will progress most rapidly with a *realistic* view of his or her chemical dependence and its effect on other people. Reality, even to an alcoholic who is abstinent, is not always self-evident. (The term "dry drunk" refers to someone who, although abstinent, is not sober or serene. This person's inappropriate or dysfunctional thinking and behavior continue in spite of not drinking.)

A user may be genuinely unaware of who has been harmed and how. When loved ones and friends join the user in treatment to detail the effects of certain actions, this is a form of intervention even though the focus is not upon entering treatment, but upon the long-term goal of recovery.

Whether it takes place before or after the user has entered a treatment program, an intervention assures the concerned persons that the user has—at last—actually heard their cries of love and pain. When the user was under the influence, they could never be sure they were heard.

Must we always *create* a crisis for the alcoholic? What about taking advantage of an existing crisis?

An existing crisis can be a golden opportunity to intervene. If, for example, an alcoholic who has been denying her problem for years has just had a serious accident while drunk, it may be best to move in immediately, rather than take time to develop the process. Just after the accident—especially if the woman is lying in a hospital bed or if she has just been fired from her job—she may be more open than she has ever been to hearing information about her drinking; information she has refused to hear in the past.

Nevertheless, the more closely the intervenors follow the process and techniques described in this book, the greater the chance of success. Observations and feelings recorded in lists or letters, rehearsed and expressed by meaningful concerned persons in a caring, nonjudgmental manner, always create the most effective approach.

When doing an intervention, how can professionals protect themselves against legal action?

Your primary client is the concerned person who comes to you for help. This client and the other concerned persons will do the actual intervention. The professional's responsibility is to assess the information gathered by the concerned persons to determine whether intervention is appropriate and, if it is, to prepare *them* to do the intervention.

It's wise for an organization—and for an individual in private practice—to show each client a written policy that clearly states the role of the professional in intervention. That policy may, for example, emphasize the professional's role as educator, evaluator, and facilitator. The policy should state that no client will be pressured to undertake intervention; that all clients must decide of their own free will. It should also include a statement about confidentiality.

To counteract any charges that the professional pressured a spouse or child to take action against her or his will, copies of the concerned persons' lists and letters can be kept in the primary client's file. Videotapes or audiotapes prepared by those who could not attend the intervention session may also be kept on file.

Being formally trained as an interventionist, and keeping professional liability coverage sufficient and up to date, will also reduce the risk of being harmed by litigation.

Legal problems rarely arise, but these preventive measures can lessen your concern about them.

Why make treatment the major focus of intervention?

The ideal form of help is primary treatment (inpatient or outpatient) at a reputable facility. Other options include group therapy or counseling by a Certified Chemical Dependence Specialist; also Twelve-Step recovery groups such as Alcoholics Anonymous, Cocaine Anonymous, or Narcotics Anonymous.

If most users attend A.A. or a similar program after treatment, why not save time and money by going there directly from the intervention session? Because Twelve-Step programs are very effective *for those who remain in the fellowship*. Receiving primary treatment before entering such a group will, we believe, increase the probability that the chemically dependent person will stay in the fellowship and fully recover.

What are the qualities of an excellent treatment program?

A good treatment program—

• Will have a qualified, licensed staff of Certified Chemical Dependence Specialists[6]

• Will devote sufficient time to evaluation, so that staff can determine with certainty whether the problem of alcohol/drug use is actually chemical dependence

• Will conduct an evaluation that's intense and powerful, so that the sheer amount of information gained, along with keen observations by other patients and the guidance of experienced and professional staff, will break through the defenses that remain after the structured intervention and will convince the user to complete the program

• Will integrate the philosophy and steps of Alcoholics Anonymous

• Will have a clearly defined family counseling program to parallel the program for the patient; preferably a program that includes close friends as well

• Will have an aftercare program not only for the patient, but also for family members and for close friends who wish to carry through

• Will, compared with other programs, have a high percentage of clients (people who have gone

---

[6] See Appendix B, *Johnson Institute Standards for Professional Interventionists.*

through treatment) still recovering—rather than using again—after one year, two years, five years, and ten years

What if the intervention doesn't work? What will I tell the family and other concerned persons?

If the user refuses help and won't even agree to a "what if" clause, *tell your clients not to give up*. They need to keep trying. The user's very life will probably depend on their continuing to describe their observations and feelings about how the drinking or other drug use is affecting them.

Stress the importance of following through with the commitments they made to themselves, for themselves, during their planning for intervention. (See *Have participants decide exactly what they will do if the user rejects all forms of help*, in Chapter 1. See also *Helping the concerned persons process the content of the session and make decisions about their future*, in Chapter 2.)

Assure the concerned persons that intervention has a cumulative effect. If the first structured intervention session does not motivate the user to accept treatment, the second one probably will—or the third one or the fourth one will. Sometimes it takes a great deal of effort to break through the user's system of denial and delusion.

Alcoholics Anonymous aptly states, "There are men and women who are constitutionally incapable of being honest with themselves. ... They are not at fault; they seem to have been born that way. They are naturally incapable of grasping and developing a manner of living which demands rigorous honesty."

And so, what about the "incorrigible" alcoholic/addict, or the one who walks out of the structured intervention and never comes back, or the one who is "too far gone" for help? If that person continues drinking/using and never gets help—or even dies—has intervention failed? The answer is *no*. In fact, according to Dr. Vernon E. Johnson, originator of the intervention process, **Properly done, intervention works every time. Properly done, there are no failures.** Here are some reasons why:

- Those who have intervened are forever changed. They know they are not alone. They know that help is available.

- The family system has changed. Whereas it used to be immobilized, fearful, guilty, shame-ridden, and otherwise dysfunctional, it is now open, honest, caring, self-respecting, able to set boundaries, and dedicated to recovery. With new understanding of chemical dependence, family members are able to recognize its symptoms in themselves. They know how to get help for themselves.

- The chemically dependent person has also changed. There is a crack in the wall of defenses. No longer can the user completely deny reality. Drinking/using will never again be enjoyed in the same way. As one family member put it, "At least we spoiled his drinking!"

Intervention always has *some* effect, and that effect is nearly always positive. At the very least it offers a chance for recovery where none existed before. At most it starts the entire family on the path toward fully living again.

AFTERWORD

God, grant me the serenity to accept the
things I cannot change,
Courage to change the things I can,
And wisdom to know the difference.

For many years *The Serenity Prayer*[1] has given millions of
members of Alcoholics Anonymous, Al-Anon, and other
self-help groups a foundation for daily living. The prayer is
clearly a work of inspiration. Everyone who reads it can
say, "Yes, yes. If I could do that, my life would be happy, my
days would flow smoothly, my heart would be at peace."

This brief invocation has as much to do with courage
and wisdom as it does with serenity. Serenity comes to
most of us only *after* we have done all we can; only *after*
we have faced our problems and examined our strengths
and weaknesses; only *after* we have make the changes in
our lives that may calm the tempest and bring us peace.

For those living with a chemically dependent
person, serenity seldom comes before action—action to
change *whatever needs to be changed and can be*
changed in their lives. To distinguish what needs to be
done and what can be done, and then to take action,
indeed takes wisdom and courage. This is where helping-
professionals can assist.

We cannot give our clients wisdom, of course. But we
can help them acquire knowledge, see new perspectives,

---

[1] *The Serenity Prayer*, by Reinhold Niebuhr, appears in many forms. One, claimed
to have been written for a service at the Congregational Church of Heath,
Massachusetts, in 1943, is, "God, give us grace to accept with serenity the things
that cannot be changed, courage to change the things which should be changed,
and the wisdom to distinguish the one from the other."

and gain insight. We can help them examine their lives and the influences on their lives so they can take action with greater awareness. We can help them see the choices they face and encourage them to make healthy, constructive decisions.

Nor can we give our clients courage. But we can help them examine their fears, trace those fears to the roots, determine how realistic they are, and decide how to overcome them. We can help free our clients from the paralyzing feelings of guilt and shame that keep them bound in painful and harmful codependent relationships. We can help them see that courage does not come all at once, but rather in small increments. With each new bit of understanding, our clients do gradually see that change is possible and that action is necessary. They try one small step, then another. When they discover that their lives haven't fallen apart, they feel encouraged to try bigger and bigger steps, with greater frequency.

Serenity comes to them when they know they have done all they can; when they know they have acted with courage and compassion; when they know they have reached out to others and have gratefully accepted the help and support their families and communities have to offer; and when they know they have dug deep within themselves and found their own resources and strength.

The helping-professional is an intermediary in this process. We do what we can to help those living with chemically dependent persons to draw upon their own potential for wisdom, courage, and serenity. We facilitate a process that their own intellectual, emotional, social, and spiritual resources will bring to fruition. Our role in intervention, then, reflects the saying,

I bind their wounds; God heals them.

Feeling Chart[1]

In presenting the *Feeling Chart*, Dr. Vernon E. Johnson says, "Most people, when they come down with a disease, will set about trying to find treatment for it, provided that medical help is available to them. Here is where chemical dependence distinguishes itself as a disease unlike any other. *The people who have it generally do not seek treatment of their own volition because they are not aware that they have it.* This is because chemical dependence is universally accompanied by an *emotional syndrome* that is unique to it and effectively blocks the consciousness that it exists." Here is a condensed version of the *Feeling Chart*. The X represents the starting point of each phase.

The Four Phases of Chemical Dependence

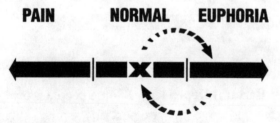

Phase I: Learning Mood Swing. As people first use alcohol or another mind-altering drug, they discover that the chemical changes how they feel—usually in a positive

[1] From Johnson, Vernon E., D.D. *Intervention: How to Help Someone Who Doesn't Want Help*. Minneapolis:Johnson Institute, 1986, pp. 16–34. Used with permission of the author. For a full explanation, please refer to Dr. Johnson's book. It's listed in Appendix C, *Johnson Institute Resources for Programming*.

way. For most people this is a pleasant experience. When the effects wear off, the user returns to normal.

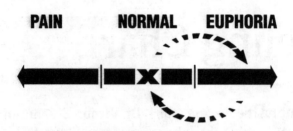

Phase II: Seeking Mood Swing. After several experiences with alcohol or other drugs, people move out of the learning stage into the seeking stage. They know what the alcohol or other drug will do, and they know how much they need in order to obtain a certain effect. Some people at this stage use the chemical to rid themselves of uncomfortable feelings, such as anger, fear, sadness, loneliness, or even joy. But the uncomfortable feelings return when the effects of the chemical wear off.

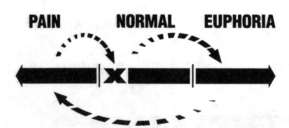

Phase III: Harmful Dependence. Some people move from the seeking stage into the next one, which signals the presence of chemical dependence. A person at this stage has lost the ability to choose whether or not to use. Up to this point, the person could select from various ways to deal with painful feelings; but now he or she relies on just one: relief through alcohol and/or other drugs. The user is no longer in control; the chemical is.

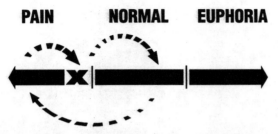

Phase IV: Using to Feel Normal. This last stage is a dangerous place, with deterioration in all areas of life—work, mental health, physical health, and human relationships. Depression is typical. People at this stage always feel bad. They use alcohol and other drugs in an attempt to feel normal again. When they reach this stage of chemical dependence, nearly everyone around them can see there is a problem.

Johnson Institute Standards for the Professional Interventionist

The qualified, professional interventionist—

1. Uses generally accepted criteria and procedures for assessing problems of chemical dependence[1]

2. Demonstrates the necessary ability (knowledge and skill) for assessing the physical, emotional, and mental capabilities of concerned persons to carry out an intervention

3. Demonstrates commitment to the Johnson Institute principle that the goal of intervention is, first and foremost, to secure immediate help for the chemically dependent person

4. Demonstrates commitment to the Johnson Institute principle that pre-intervention counseling for concerned persons is short-term and time-limited and should not be prolonged to an extent that causes help for the chemically dependent person to be postponed

---

[1] Such as those approved by the National Council on Alcoholism and Drug Dependence (NCADD)

5. Ensures that during an intervention, statements by concerned persons to the chemically dependent person are not shaming or demeaning but are caring and respectful, describing specific facts and feelings

6. Treats all persons in the intervention process with care and concern, and works to preserve the dignity and self-respect of the chemically dependent person

7. Demonstrates a commitment to helping families by directing all family members involved in an intervention into their own process of recovery

8. Has completed a Johnson Institute-approved training and certification process for professional interventionists

NOTE: To find out how to become a member of the National Intervention Network, write the National Council on Alcoholism and Drug Dependence (NCADD) at 12 West 21st Street, New York, NY 10010. Or phone (212) 206-6770, extension 19.

Johnson Institute Resources for Programming

The following materials are available from the Johnson Institute. Call toll-free at 800-231-5165 for ordering information, current prices, or a complete guide to Johnson Institute resources.

Kits

Family Intervention Primer. Order #V408KIT.
  Including—

  Video, *Back to Reality*, featuring Hugh Downs; 31 minutes
  Book, *Intervention: How to Help Someone Who Doesn't Want Help*
  Workbook, *Recovery Is a Family Affair: How You Can Help and Feel Good About It*

Kit items are also listed separately below.

Video Programs

Back to Reality: What We Need to Know to Conquer Addiction.
(3-part video series). Order #V408S

> *Back to Reality.* 31 minutes. Order #V408
> *Enabling: Masking Reality.* 22 minutes. Order #V409
> *Intervention: Facing Reality.* 30 minutes. Order #V410

Choices & Consequences: Intervention with Youth in Trouble with Alcohol/Drugs. 33 minutes. Order #V400

Intervention: How to Help Someone Who Doesn't Want Help. 48 minutes. Order #V406

Books

Cermak, Timmen L., M.D. *Diagnosing and Treating Co-dependence: A Guide for Professionals Who Work with Chemical Dependents, Their Spouses and Children.* Order #P100

Johnson, Vernon E., D.D. *Intervention: How to Help Someone Who Doesn't Want Help.* Order #P140

Leite, Evelyn, and Pamela Espeland. *Different Like Me: A Book for Teens Who Worry About Their Parents' Use of Alcohol/Drugs.* Order #P097

Schaefer, Dick. *Choices & Consequences: What to Do When a Teenager Uses Alcohol/Drugs. A Step-by-Step System That Really Works.* Rev. Ed. Order #P096

Workbooks

*How to Get Sober, Stay Sober, and Feel Good About It —
Steps 1, 2, and 3.* An easy-to-follow learning process that
takes the participant through the first three steps of the
recovery process. Order #P264

*How to Get Sober, Stay Sober, and Feel Good About It—
Steps 4 and 5.* Leads the participant further on the
journey toward recovery. Order #P265

Recovery Is a Family Affair. Helps family members
understand how their loved one's addiction has affected
them. Order #P266

Recovery Series Booklets

Twelve-Step Series

Step One: Facing the Problem. Order #P005-1

Step Two: Becoming Spiritual. Order #P005-2

Step Three: Becoming Willing. Order #P005-3

Steps Four and Five: Becoming Honest. Order #P005-
4&5

Steps Six and Seven: Becoming Ready and Humble.
Order #P005-6&7

Steps Eight and Nine: Making Amends. #P005-8&9

Steps Ten Through Twelve: Maintaining Sobriety.
#P005-10:12

Anger: How to Handle It During Recovery. Order #P017

Behavior vs. Values: Character Conflict During Recovery. Order #P004

Chemical Dependence and Recovery: A Family Affair. Order #P104

Chemical Dependence: Yes, You Can Do Something. Order #P099

Detachment vs. Intervention: Is There a Conflict? Order #P033

Getting Reconnected: Improving Relationships with Yourself and Others. Order #P188

God, Help Me to Be Me: Spiritual Growth During Recovery. Order #P006

Index

References are to page numbers.

A.A. *See* Alcoholics Anonymous
Absent intervenors, 15, 66, 86, 93, 102, 107, 125–126
Abstinence
    as condition of treatment, 42
    "dry drunk", 128
Abuse, emotional/physical/sexual, 45, 70, 113, 122
Abusers, intervention with, 123
Adapting intervention
    for absent intervenors, 15, 125–26
    for various populations, 51, 119–120, 121–122, 123–124
Adult Children of Alcoholics, 66, 119
Adolescents, intervention with, 123–124
Aftercare. *See* Follow-through
Age of intervenors, 15, 19, 60, 103
Al-Anon, 48, 66, 102, 123, 126–127
Alateen, 66
Alcoholics Anonymous, 17, 49, 66, 130
Alcoholism. *See* Chemical dependence; Warning signs of chemical dependence
Amnesia. *See* Warning signs of chemical dependence: blackouts
Anger
    not in confrontation, 9–10, 19, 21, 84

upsetting expectation of, 21, 23
    See also Feelings
Apologies, 11
Assessment
    preliminary, 52–57
    self-report, 42, 48
    vs. diagnosis, 56, 60, 75
Audiotape of presentation, 15, 19, 126
Awareness, lack of, 35, 62, 137

Blackouts. *See* Warning signs of chemical dependence
Blaming, 22, 36, 62
Business executives, intervention with, 122

CAST. *See Children of Alcoholics Screening Test*
CEOs, intervention with, 122
Certified Chemical Dependence Specialist, 75, 130, 131
Chemical dependence
    assessment, 42, 48, 52–57, 60
    as disease, 2, 61–63, 103, 137–139
    as weakness, 15, 62, 110
    codependent's own, 112–113
    discovered during counseling, 48–49
    genetic influence, 63, 100
    helping-professional's own, 49, 122
    intervenor's own, 57, 66, 68

147

ORDER FORM

<table>
<tr><td>

BILL TO:

Name _____

Address _____

_____

City _____ State _____ Zip _____

ATTENTION: _____

Daytime Phone: ( ) _____

PURCHASE ORDER NO. _____

☐ Individual Order   ☐ Group or Organization Order

Ordering for a Group or Organization:

Group Name _____

</td><td>

SHIP TO: (if different from BILL TO)

Name _____

Address _____

_____

City _____ State _____ Zip _____

ATTENTION: _____

Daytime Phone: ( ) _____

TAX EXEMPT NO. _____

</td></tr>
</table>

| Please send me a free copy(ies) of Johnson Institute's: | ☐ __ Publications and Films Catalog
 ☐ __ Training Calendar(s)
 ☐ *Observer*, a quarterly newsletter |

PLEASE SEND ME:

QTY.	ORDER NO.	TITLE	PRICE EACH	TOTAL COST

For film/video titles, please specify: ☐ 1/2" VHS   ☐ 3/4" U-Matic   ☐ 1/2" Beta   ☐ 16mm

SHIPPING AND HANDLING

Order Amount	U.S.	Outside U.S.
0–25.00	$ 6.50	$8.00
25.01–60.00	$ 8.50	$10.00
60.01–130.00	$10.50	$13.50
130.01–200.00	$13.25	$19.50
200.01–300.00	$16.00	$24.00
300.01–over	8%	14%

Please add $8.00 ($10.50 Canada) for any videotapes ordered.

OFFICE USE ONLY

Order No. _____

Customer No. _____

VS, Inc.

☐ Payment enclosed
☐ Bill me
☐ Bill my credit card:

☐ MasterCard
☐ VISA
☐ American Express
☐ Discover

[ ][ ][ ][ ][ ][ ][ ][ ][ ][ ][ ][ ][ ][ ][ ][ ][ ]

Expiration Date: _____

Signature on card: _____

Total Order _____
(Orders under $75.00 must be prepaid)

6.5% Sales Tax _____
(Minnesota Residents Only)

Shipping and Handling _____
(See Chart)

TOTAL _____

Have you ordered from the Johnson Institute before? Yes ☐   No ☐
If yes, how?   Mail ☐   Phone ☐

JOHNSON INSTITUTE®

7205 Ohms Lane ✦ Minneapolis, Minnesota 55439-2159
(612) 831-1630 or toll-free: 1-800-231-5165